The Heart of Higher Education: A Call to Renewal

TRANSFORMING THE ACADEMY THROUGH COLLEGIAL CONVERSATIONS

Parker J. Palmer and Arthur Zajonc, with Megan Scribner

Foreword by
Mark Nepo

JOSSEY-BASS
A Wiley Imprint
www.josseybass.com

The Jossey-Bass
Higher and Adult Education Series

Published by Jossey-Bass
A Wiley Imprint
989 Market Street, San Francisco, CA 94103-1741—www.josseybass.com

Jossey-Bass books and products are available through most bookstores. To contact Jossey-Bass directly call our Customer Care Department within the U.S. at 800-956-7739, outside the U.S. at 317-572-3986, or fax 317-572-4002.

Jossey-Bass also publishes its books in a variety of electronic formats. Some content that appears in print may not be available in electronic books.

Library of Congress Cataloging-in-Publication Data

Palmer, Parker J.
  The heart of higher education : a call to renewal / Parker J. Palmer and Arthur Zajonc with Megan Scribner ; foreword by Mark Nepo.
    p. cm.
  Includes bibliographical references and index.
  ISBN 978-0-470-48790-7 (hardback)
  1. Education, Higher--Philosophy. 2. Educational change. 3. Educational innovations. I. Zajonc, Arthur. II. Scribner, Megan. III. Title.
  LB2322.2.P35 2010
  378.01--dc22

2010013825

Printed in the United States of America
FIRST EDITION
HB Printing 10 9 8 7 6 5 4 3 2 1

Contents

Foreword

The issues facing the next generation globally demand that
we educate our students worldwide to use all of their
resources, not just their mind or their heart. The hour is late,
the work is hard, and the stakes are high, but few institutions
are better positioned to take up this work than our nation's
colleges and universities.[1]

— Diana Chapman Walsh,
President Emerita, Wellesley College

What you have before you is a thoughtful and grounded invitation to live into the heart of higher education and to deepen our understanding and practice of transformative learning. The magnitude of the issues confronting the world requires whole people with whole minds and hearts to lead us into tomorrow. And that, in turn, requires us to renew the human purpose and meaning at the heart of higher education.

Parker Palmer and Arthur Zajonc have devoted their lives to creating forms of education that serve the human cause. Their book arrives at a critical and creative juncture in the evolution of higher education in the emerging global community. In particular, this book is an affirming response to an unprecedented international higher education conference held in 2007 and funded by the Fetzer Institute. Rather than a compendium of the worthwhile papers, presentations, and dialogues offered at the conference, this book is a call to the growing interest and commitment to integrative education that the conference signified.

After two years of planning, the conference, "Uncovering the Heart of Higher Education: Integrative Learning for Compassionate Action in an Interconnected World," was held in San Francisco, February 22–25, 2007. The conference drew over six hundred educators, administrators, student life professionals, chaplains, and students, representing 260 institutions from North America and around the world—from Schenectady High School in upstate New York to the University of Cape Town in South Africa, and from the University of British Columbia in Canada to Richland Community College in Dallas, Texas.

Partnering organizations who helped convene this unique gathering included the Asian Art Museum of San Francisco, the Associated New American Colleges, the Association of American Colleges and Universities, the Center for Courage & Renewal, the Contemplative Mind in Society, the Council of Independent Colleges, the League for Innovation in the Community Colleges, the National Association of Student Personnel Administrators, and Naropa University.

Our primary partner and host institution for this conference was the California Institute of Integral Studies (CIIS). A special gratitude goes out to our warm colleagues at CIIS, to the president of CIIS, Joseph Subbiondo, for his vision and leadership, and to my Fetzer colleague Deborah Higgins for her devotion and excellence. Without their effort and care, this remarkable conference would never have happened. And deep gratitude to Megan Scribner, whose gift as a thinking partner and editor helped knit the compelling questions of the conference and the rich voices of the authors into the book you have before you.

I must confess that standing in the midst of such a remarkable community of educators for that one week in San Francisco triggered an awareness that a healthy conversation is alive and well among educators around the world. The fundamental questions at the center of this growing conversation and at the center of the conference can be offered as: Do current education efforts address the whole human being—mind, heart, and spirit—in ways that best contribute to our future on this fragile planet? What steps can we take to make our colleges and universities places that awaken the deepest potential in students, faculty, and staff? How can integrative learning be effectively woven into the culture, curriculum, and co-curriculum of our colleges and universities? These questions remain active guideposts for ongoing work in higher education.

The Fetzer Institute has had a long-term commitment to holistic education. Over the last fifteen years, the Institute has actively encouraged the development of a vital conversation between education and spirituality that is prompted by the recognition that education, especially higher education, serves as an incubator of intellectual and professional life that cannot rightly be sheared from the formation of the whole person and his or her interdependence with the wider world. Fetzer has both responded to and encouraged the art and practice of transformational education as integral to the central and best purposes of higher education.

Transformational education—understood as educating the whole person by integrating the inner life and the outer life, by actualizing individual and global awakening, and by participating in compassionate communities—has become a quiet but sturdy movement that encourages the recovery and development of the academy as a liberating and capacity-building environment. Much work, however, remains as higher education is in great flux; outcomes aligned with the aspirations of transformative education are by no means clear or guaranteed, thus the need for this book and the threshold it represents for this much-needed conversation to continue.

ENTER WITH YOUR OWN GIFT

Vocation is the place
where the heart's deep gladness
meets the world's deep hunger.

— ADAPTED FROM FREDERICK BUECHNER

What does it mean to balance educating the mind with educating the heart? In terms of action in the world, it suggests that a tool is only as good as the hand that guides it, and the guiding hand is only as wise and compassionate as the mind and heart that direct it. The heart of higher education has something to do with connecting all the meaningful parts of being human and the increasingly important challenge of how we live together in our time on earth.

Blair Ruble, director of the Comparative Urban Studies Project at the Woodrow Wilson Center for International Scholars, tells us:

> We live in a world that is different from that inhabited by our ancestors in many profound ways. According to the United Nations, the global urban population in 2008 has reached 3.3 billion people, more than half of all humans living on the planet. This reality stands in contrast to 13 percent a century ago; and 3 percent a century before that.[2]

Implicit in this shift in the human landscape is the increasing importance of compassion and community, as the future will demand even more skill and grace in the art of living together. And so, the urban press of the future is one more reason that the heart of higher education needs to liberate individuals' capacity for compassion and community and provide them with the skillful means to inhabit these capacities.

Certainly everyone doesn't have the opportunity to experience higher education, but a significant and growing percentage of young people around the world make their way to college: at least twenty million annually in the United States, which contributes to the forty million globally each year. This means that higher education is the developmental home for enough young lives to fully populate the cities of New York, Shanghai, and Los Angeles combined, *every year*.

Consider then that for each generation there is a developmental window from approximately the ages of eighteen to thirty-five in which these capacities for compassion and community can be awakened. These ages happen to correspond to the span of under-graduate education, graduate education, and professional schools such as medicine or law. Within this context, the individual's journey through higher education, if made meaningful, holds a crucial turning point which Harvard researcher Robert Kegan describes as the movement from the individual, personal mind to the social, relational mind. He suggests , in fact, that higher education's chief responsibility is to foster this transformation from independence to interdependence.

The depth and clarity of this book helps us begin the search for how our gifts as educators can help foster this transformation and meet the world's deep hunger that keeps calling for our own compassion and community. The fertile ground opened here helps us to realize a deep and timeless call inherent to all education—to enliven and affirm fully compassionate and skilled people who can take their place in the global human family.

The French writer Alexis de Tocqueville came to the United States during the 1830s to chronicle the character of a new nation. In *Democracy in America,* he defined and described the "habits of the heart" that vitalized the experiment called America. Today, we are learning that the habits of the heart are not just American but at the deepest level human. Therefore, it is the responsibility of humanity as a whole to incubate and cultivate this vitality of heart. As the Dalai Lama has said, "There is a need to develop a secular ethics of the heart. This is a question with important implications for fostering the ideals of community, compassion, and cooperation in our homes, public institutions, and society."[3]

To develop a secular ethics of the heart, a reclamation of educational purpose is necessary. With this in mind, consider the interesting conundrum that the legendary researchers Sandy and Helen Astin of UCLA observed through six years of survey research regarding spirituality and higher education. After they surveyed over 1,200 undergraduates and over 800 faculty from over eighty different institutions, a startling insight surfaced. When asked, almost 80 percent of both undergraduates and faculty said that they considered themselves spiritual and that they were committed to a search for purpose and meaning. When asked how often they experienced such a search in the classroom, almost 60 percent of both undergraduates and faculty reported never. Since the overwhelming majority of faculty and students have the interpersonal and collective power to shape their classroom experiences, this alarming discrepancy raises the disturbing and yet hopeful question: Who's stopping us? What imagined, habitual, or real barriers are preventing our educational communities from actualizing meaningful dialogues around spirit, purpose, and transformation?

Regardless of what role you may play in the world of education—as a teacher, an administrator, a student-life professional, a chaplain, or a student—we invite you into greater reflection, dialogue, and commitment to uncover and inhabit this vital and renewable heart of higher education.

Both of these authors invite us with honest and gentle rigor into deeper realms of what this heart of higher education might contain. Parker opens the door of integrative learning when he says:

> We are being called into a more paradoxical wholeness of
> knowing by many voices. There is a new community of
> scholars in a variety of fields now who understand that genuine
> knowing comes out of a healthy dance between the objective
> and the subjective, between the analytic and the integrative,
> between the experimental and what I would call the receptive.
> So, I am not trying to split these paradoxes apart; I am trying to
> put them back together.

And Arthur challenges us to walk through that door when he says:

> If I were to ask, What should be at the center of our teaching
> and our student's learning, what would you respond? Of the
> many tasks that we as educators take up, what, in your view, is
> the most important task of all? What is our greatest hope for

the young people we teach? In his letters to the young poet Franz Kappus, Rainer Maria Rilke answered unequivocally: "To take love seriously and to bear and to learn it like a task, this is what [young] people need .... For one human being to love another, that is perhaps the most difficult of all our tasks, the ultimate, the last test and proof, the work for which all other work is but a preparation. For this reason young people, who are beginners in everything, cannot yet know love; they have to learn it. With their whole being, with all their forces, gathered close about their lonely, timid, upward-beating heart, they must learn to love."

Need I say it? The curricula offered by our institutions of higher education have largely neglected this central, if profoundly difficult task of learning to love, which is also the task of learning to live in true peace and harmony with others and with nature.

As a lifelong teacher, I find these questions and invitations life-sustaining. In a meaningful way, this book asks, again, Just what is the realm of the responsible teacher? However you are drawn to hold this question, the question alone presumes a devoted engagement which is necessary because true education is messy, never clear, and the lessons shift and the boundaries change.

Let me share a recent teachable moment. I was in Prague. There, in our last workshop, we invited people to tell the story of a small kindness that helped them know their true self. We asked people to be quiet and still for thirty seconds in order to let that act of kindness find them. Later, a researcher from Holland spoke tenderly of a moment five years earlier. She was reading alone in her home and night fell and the room grew very dark. She just kept reading and, suddenly and quietly, her husband appeared with a lamp to help her see. Her small moment touched me at the core. For isn't this a metaphor for the promise of all education, how the smallest light will fill every corner of a dark room? Isn't the lamp we carry from darkness to darkness our very heart?

In conclusion, I believe in this book, I believe in these authors, I believe in the promise that higher education holds. I believe in the lamp of the heart. This book, and all it comes from and all it points to, is such a lamp.

—Mark Nepo
Program Officer
Fetzer Institute

Gratitudes

We are grateful to all the people without whom this book would never have seen the light of day. We must begin by acknowledging that our collaboration has deepened the friendship that began years back, and that each of us has treasured the insights and teachings the other has brought to the book and to the subject of integrative education. We also thank our editor, colleague, and friend, Megan Scribner, who is thoughtful and thorough in her work and laughs a lot as she does it; our friends at the Fetzer Institute, especially Mark Nepo, who launched this project and helped set its trajectory; the 600-plus people who came to San Francisco in February of 2007 and generated the creative force field that emerged from the conference "Uncovering the Heart of Higher Education"; Joe Subbiondo, president of the California Institute of Integral Studies, who, along with his dedicated staff, helped make that conference a success; and David Brightman, our supportive editor at Jossey-Bass.

The question "Who and what are you grateful for as this book goes to press?" takes us down memory lane—which, at our stage of life, is more like hiking the Appalachian Trail end to end than taking an afternoon ramble. The best we can do here is to thank the many people in many places who enlivened and encouraged our vision of integrative education over the years as students, teachers, and writers, roles we are grateful to be playing to this day.

—Parker J. Palmer and Arthur Zajonc

The Authors

Parker J. Palmer is a highly respected writer, teacher, and activist who focuses on issues in education, community, leadership, spirituality, and social change. His work speaks deeply to people in many walks of life, including public schools, colleges and universities, religious institutions, corporations, foundations, and grassroots organizations.

Palmer served for fifteen years as senior associate of the American Association of Higher Education. He now serves as senior adviser to the Fetzer Institute. He founded the Center for Courage & Renewal (www.couragerenewal.org), which oversees the Courage to Teach program for K–12 educators across the country and parallel programs for people in other professions, including medicine, law, ministry, and philanthropy.

He has published a dozen poems, more than one hundred essays, and seven books, including several best-selling and award-winning titles: *A Hidden Wholeness, Let Your Life Speak, The Courage to Teach, The Active Life, To Know as We Are Known, The Company of Strangers,* and *The Promise of Paradox.*

Palmer's work has been recognized with ten honorary doctorates, two Distinguished Achievement Awards from the National Educational Press Association, an Award of Excellence from the Associated Church Press, and major grants from the Danforth Foundation, the Lilly Endowment, and the Fetzer Institute.

In 1993, Palmer won the national award of the Council of Independent Colleges for Outstanding Contributions to Higher Education. In 1998, the Leadership Project, a national survey of ten thousand administrators and faculty, named Palmer one of the thirty "most influential senior leaders" in higher education and one of the ten key "agenda setters" of the 1990s: "He has inspired a generation of teachers and reformers with evocative visions of community, knowing, and spiritual wholeness."

In 2001, Carleton College gave Palmer the Distinguished Alumni Achievement Award. The following year, the Accreditation Council for Graduate Medical Education created the Parker J. Palmer Courage to Teach Award, given annually to the directors of ten medical residency programs that exemplify patient-centered professionalism in medical education. A year later, the American College Personnel Association named Palmer its Diamond Honoree for outstanding contributions to the field of student affairs.

In 2005, Jossey-Bass published *Living the Questions: Essays Inspired by the Work and Life of Parker J. Palmer,* written by notable practitioners in a variety of fields including medicine, law, philanthropy, politics, economic development, K–12, and higher education.

Parker J. Palmer received his Ph.D. in sociology from the University of California at Berkeley. A member of the Religious Society of Friends (Quaker), he lives with his wife, Sharon Palmer, in Madison, Wisconsin.

Arthur Zajonc is professor of physics at Amherst College, where he has taught since 1978. He received his B.S. and Ph.D. in physics from the University of Michigan. He has been visiting professor and research scientist at the Ecole Normale Superieure in Paris, the Max Planck Institute for Quantum Optics, and the universities of Rochester and Hanover. He has been a Fulbright professor at the University of Innsbruck in Austria. His research has included studies in electron-atom physics, parity violation in atoms, quantum optics, the experimental foundations of quantum physics, and the relationship between science, the humanities, and the contemplative traditions. He has written extensively on Goethe's science work. He is author of *Catching the Light* (Bantam & Oxford University Press), co-author of *The Quantum Challenge* (Jones & Bartlett), and co-editor of *Goethe's Way of Science* (SUNY Press).

In 1997 he served as scientific coordinator for the Mind and Life dialogue published as *The New Physics and Cosmology: Dialogues with the Dalai Lama* (Oxford University Press). He again organized the 2002 dialogue with the Dalai Lama, "The Nature of Matter, the Nature of Life," and acted as moderator at MIT for the "Investigating the Mind" Mind and Life dialogue in 2003. The proceedings of the Mind and Life–MIT meeting were published under the title *The Dalai Lama at MIT* (Harvard University Press), which he co-edited.

Most recently he is author of *Meditation as Contemplative Inquiry: When Knowing Becomes Love* (Lindisfarne Press) on contemplative pedagogy and a volume on the youth program PeaceJam, *We Speak as One: Twelve Nobel Laureates Share Their Vision for Peace.* He currently is an advisor to the World Future Council and directs the Academic Program of the Center for Contemplative Mind in Society, which supports appropriate inclusion of contemplative methods in higher education. He was also a cofounder of the Kira Institute, general secretary of the Anthroposophical Society, president/chair of the Lindisfarne Association, and a senior program director at the Fetzer Institute.

Megan Scribner is an editor, writer, and researcher who has documented and evaluated projects for nonprofits for almost thirty years. She is coeditor of *Leading from Within: Poetry That Sustains the Courage to Lead* and *Teaching with Fire: Poetry That Sustains the Courage to Teach* and editor of *Navigating the Terrain of Childhood: A Guide for Meaningful Parenting and Heartfelt Discipline.* She also coauthored with Parker J. Palmer *The Courage to Teach Guide for Reflection and Renewal, Tenth Anniversary Edition.* She has edited discussion guides, such as the one published by the World Resource Institute to accompany the *Bill Moyers Reports: Earth on Edge* video. She also coedited *Transformations of Myth Through Time: An*

Anthology of Readings and the *Joseph Campbell Transformations of Myth Through Time Study Guide,* as well as coauthored the project's *Faculty and Administrator's Manual.*

In addition to her writing and editing, Scribner is an advisor with the Fetzer Institute and has evaluated a number of renewal and leadership programs with Smith College Professor Sam Intrator. Scribner received her master's degree in American Studies from George Washington University. She lives with her husband, Bruce Kozarsky, and their two daughters, Anya and Maya Kozarsky, in Takoma Park, Maryland.

Introduction

Parker J. Palmer and Arthur Zajonc

> The thing being made in a university is humanity. . . . [W]hat universities . . . are *mandated* to make or to help to make is human beings in the fullest sense of those words—not just trained workers or knowledgeable citizens but responsible heirs and members of human culture. . . . Underlying the idea of a university—the bringing together, the combining into one, of all the disciplines—is the idea that good work and good citizenship are the inevitable by-products of the making of a good—that is, a fully developed—human being.[1]
>
> — WENDELL BERRY

This book emerged from a long series of conversations between its co-authors, their close colleagues, and many others—the kind of conversations that bring people closer to the heart of a shared concern, give them new eyes to see both the problems and possibilities, and set the stage for taking creative action.

1

Like many educators we know, we went to college seeking not only knowledge but a sense of meaning and purpose for our lives. Both of us had good teachers who helped along those lines, and we aspired to become teachers of that sort. But early on in our academic careers, we found that the disciplinary silos in which we had been educated—and the fragmentary and fragmenting assumptions about knowledge and humanity that often lay behind them—obscured as much as they revealed about the nature of reality and how to inhabit it as whole human beings. We found it increasingly difficult and frustrating to "color within the lines" as we tried to teach in ways that answer Wendell Berry's call to help students become more fully developed human beings.

Animated by our vocational passions and frustrations, both of us have felt called to work with others in helping higher education rejoin that which it too often puts asunder—for the sake of students, those who teach them, and a world that stands in need of integrative hearts and minds. We have been drawn to, and invite you to explore with us, the question at the heart of this book and the many conversations that led to it:

> How can higher education become a more multidimensional enterprise, one that draws on the full range of human capacities for knowing, teaching, and learning; that bridges the gaps between the disciplines; that forges stronger links between knowing the world and living creatively in it, in solitude and community?

If we cannot find ways to respond to that question—not with a monolithic solution, but by laying down multiple threads of inquiry and experimentation that might come together in a larger and more coherent tapestry of insight and practice—we will continue to make fleeting and fragmentary responses to the hungers and needs of our students, to the abiding questions of the human adventure, and to the social, economic, and political challenges of our time. As large as that agenda obviously is, we believe it describes the high calling of higher education, a calling embedded in its cultural and institutional DNA.

We are certainly not alone in our concerns. Many prominent commentators have authored important critiques of the way we educate students. In his book *Excellence Without a Soul,* Harry Lewis, the former dean of Harvard College, explains that "Harvard and our other great universities lost sight of the essential purpose of undergraduate education."[2] Beyond academic and research excellence, universities have forgotten their main purpose, which is to help students "learn who they are, to search for a larger purpose for their lives, and to leave college as better human beings."[3] Lamenting the shallowness of the university's response to problems within higher education, Lewis writes, "The students are not soulless, but their university is."[4] He contends that reforms, where they do take place, do not go nearly deep enough to re-ensoul the university and reestablish the purpose of higher education, which is the fostering of our full humanity.

Echoing Lewis's sentiments, former Yale Law School dean Anthony Kronman argues persuasively in *Education's End* that the true purpose of education has been lost, namely, a deep exploration concerning the meaning of life or "what life is for."[5] He goes on to write, "A college or university is not just a place for the transmission of knowledge but a forum for the exploration of life's mystery and meaning through the careful but critical reading of the great works of literary and philosophical imagination."[6] Something essential has gone missing, something that brought coherence and true purpose to our colleges and universities. It is to that absence that we direct our attention in this book.

THE ORIGINS OF THIS BOOK

In structuring this book, we have not tried to reproduce the conversations that led to it. You will not find sections where Arthur says " . . . ," and then Parker says " . . . ." Nor have we tried to meld our two voices into one by synchronizing our ways of thinking and writing, preferring to maintain the differences in voices and viewpoints that proved fruitful when we were speaking face-to-face. Instead, chapter by chapter, each of us has addressed certain aspects of the "integrative education question" in his own way. But every part of this book that is in one author's voice has been challenged, stretched, and refined in conversation with the other—indeed, with many others.

We came to this conversation about the heart of higher education from quite different directions. In fact, given the balkanization of much of academic life, we might be regarded as a conversational odd couple! But that is part of what has made the conversation so invigorating for each of us.

Arthur Zajonc studied engineering (BSE) and physics (PhD 1976) at the University of Michigan in Ann Arbor and has been a physicist, professor, and interdisciplinary scholar at Amherst College for over thirty years. Zajonc's scientific research has spanned a range of topics in atom-laser physics, but he has been especially engaged with the experimental foundations of quantum mechanics. Parallel with his laboratory research, Zajonc has had a sustained interest in the history and philosophy of science, especially in the relationship between the sciences, arts, and humanities. Since the mid-1990s he has been active in the area of integrative and transformative education for college students, with a special interest in "contemplative pedagogy."

Parker Palmer studied philosophy and sociology as an undergraduate at Carleton College, spent a year at Union Theological Seminary in New York, and received a PhD in sociology from the University of California at Berkeley in 1970. Deciding to use his sociology "in the streets" rather than in the academy, Palmer spent five years as a community organizer in the Washington, D.C., area and then lived and worked for a decade at a Quaker living-learning community for adult students and seekers. For the past twenty-five years, he has been an independent writer, traveling teacher, and educational activist, interspersing his independent work with professorships at the Union Institute and University, Georgetown University, Berea College, and Carleton College. His primary interests have been in education (especially pedagogy) at every level, community, spirituality, and social change. He is the founder of the Center for Courage & Renewal.[7]

The two of us—joined by a shared vision of the power and promise of higher education to "think ourselves and the world together" rather than contribute to the fragmentation of self and world—began talking with each other over a decade ago, thanks to the hospitality of the Fetzer Institute.[8] During these years, others have joined our conversation, or we have joined theirs, seeking the insight and skillful means necessary to encourage forms of teaching and learning that honor the complexities of reality and our multiple ways of knowing, weaving it all together in ways that contribute to personal well-being and to the common good.

Sometimes good conversations are ends in themselves, good simply because they are enjoyable and edifying. At other times, something stirs in the participants, and larger forms of dialogue and action begin to take shape. One outcome of the conversation we have participated in was a national conference funded, organized, and hosted by two of our conversation partners: Mark Nepo, program officer at the Fetzer Institute, and Joseph Subbiondo, president of the California Institute of Integral Studies.

Titled "Uncovering the Heart of Higher Education: Integrative Learning for Compassionate Action in an Interconnected World" and held in San Francisco in February 2007, the conference drew over six hundred highly engaged participants from the United States and abroad. The conference brochure posed its central question: "Do current educational efforts address the whole human being—mind, heart, and spirit—in ways that contribute best to our future on this fragile planet? How can we help our colleges and universities become places that awaken the deepest potential in students, faculty, and staff?"

Some participants came to explore methods of practicing integrative education through interdisciplinary courses, service learning projects, the integration of curricular and extracurricular activities, and so forth. Others, ourselves included, while appreciating the growing number of practical applications in the field, came to inquire into the philosophical framework of integrative education in hopes of strengthening the infrastructure that can give credibility and coherence to its many pedagogical iterations. We pursued questions such as these:

- What mental images do we carry of ourselves, our students, our colleagues, our academic fields, our world?
- What do we assume about how students learn and what they bring into the classroom? What do we assume about how we teach and what we bring into the classroom?
- What assumptions about knowledge itself undergird the dominant academic culture and our pedagogical practices?
- How might we engage those assumptions creatively toward a philosophy of education that is more supportive of integrative forms of teaching and learning?

As the conference unfolded, we felt that we were witnessing and participating in a fragmented but promising movement-in-the-making that began a long time ago and will, we hope, go on for a long time to come. It is a force field whose premises, means, and ends are not yet well formed or fully articulated, but it contains great energy on behalf of the humanization of the university, as Wendell Berry might call it.

A VERY BRIEF HISTORY
OF INTEGRATIVE EDUCATION

We did not ground this book in a tight definition of "integrative education," nor is it our goal to end up with one. That concept opens out in so many directions that an overly precise definition might replicate the problem we hope to address, reducing complexity to the kind of simplicity that conceals more than it reveals. One of the virtues of conversation, as opposed to declaration, is that you do not need a precise definition to make headway: the nuances of a good conversation allow you to probe complex problems without reducing them to single dimensions or sound bites. In launching a conversation about integrative education, one could do worse than simply take the provocative Wendell Berry quote that serves as the epigraph for this Introduction, put it before a group, and ask, "What do you think?"

That said, we want to offer a context for this discussion with a brief flyover of the history of integrative education. Integration has been an enduring goal in education for a long time. In the cathedral schools of twelfth-century Europe, the Seven Liberal Arts were, in the words of Alain de Lille, intended to produce "the good and perfect man," all of whose parts were so refined and in harmony with one another that he could make the spiritual journey to God.[9] In the intervening centuries higher education has gradually become more secular and pragmatic in its orientation, but even today the ideals of a liberal education include integration across disciplines, connection to community, and alignment of one's studies with the inner aspirations that give direction and meaning to one's life.

During the last dozen years, interest in integrative learning and teaching has been on the rise, and yet clarity as to its character, aims, and methods has been slow to emerge. In 2003 the Carnegie Foundation for the Advancement of Teaching and the Association of American Colleges and Universities (AAC&U) jointly solicited proposals for a project called "Integrative Learning: Opportunities to Connect."[10] In response, 139 colleges and universities applied. One of the most common sets of questions posed by the applicants was, What is integrative learning? How do you teach it? How do you assess it?[11] Applicants lamented the fragmentation associated with today's learning, but they clearly lacked a satisfactory understanding of what integrative learning was, or how it could be taught and assessed. As one recent conference announcement on integrative learning expressed it: "What are the hallmarks of integrative learning? What are its aims and purposes? How does it help students move past fragmentation and develop a sense of motivation and purpose in the world?"[12]

Ten colleges and universities were selected to participate in the Integrative Learning Project in order to "develop and access advanced models and strategies to help students pursue learning in more intentional, connected ways." The valuable fruits of that project in the areas of curriculum, pedagogy, faculty development, and assessment are available on the project website.[13]

In its "Statement on Integrative Learning," the AAC&U rightly observes that "Integrative learning comes in many varieties: connecting skills and knowledge from multiple sources and experiences; applying theory to practice in various settings; utilizing diverse and even contradictory points of view; and, understanding issues and positions contextually."[14] This characterization covers a lot of ground and seems to us a sound generalization of the diverse efforts that have been made toward integration. If one surveys the multitude of responses educators have made to the fragmentation of learning, patterns do arise. The prevalent way of viewing integrative learning is as modification of the undergraduate curriculum and instruction to include greater explicit connection between

- courses within the major
- courses in the major and other courses beyond the major
- curricular and co-curricular activities, including community engagement

These goals can be implemented by a wide array of techniques such as linked courses, general education and capstone courses, service learning, team teaching, first-year experiences, and learning communities. In order for such strategies to work, faculty needs to practice integrative methods of instruction and student assessment, which in turn necessitates faculty development as well as institutional support and incentives.

The concept map in Figure 1 offers an overview of the ways in which curriculum development, faculty development, and assessment all contribute to integrative learning.

Another take on our theme can be found in the volume on integral education edited by Esbjörn-Hargens, Reams, and Gunnlaugson.[15] They identify many sources for this approach to teaching and learning, ranging from ancient philosophical and spiritual traditions to transpersonal psychology and the work of Ken

Figure 1. *Integrative Learning Concept Map*

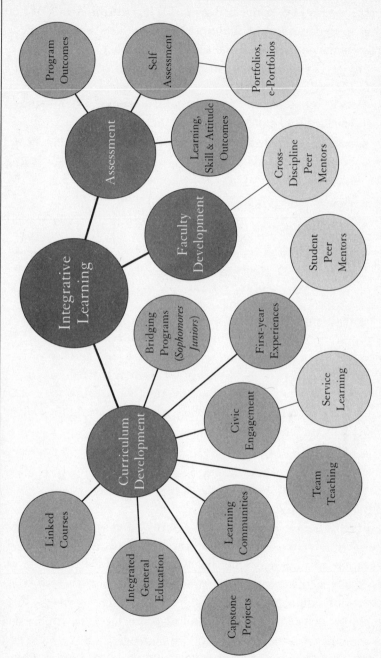

Source: Jeremy Kemp, "Integrative Learning Concept Map," *Wikipedia,* http://en.wikipedia.org/wiki/File:Integrative_learning _concept_map.gif (accessed December 17, 2009). Based on M. T. Huber, P. Hutchings, & R. Gale, "Integrative Learning for Liberal Education," *peerReview* (Summer / Fall 2005).

Wilber, grounding the recent origins of integral education in the spiritual philosophy of the Indian writer Sri Aurobindo.[16] While eschewing a definition of integral education, they enumerate the characteristics of learning and teaching within that model:

- exploring multiple perspectives
- including first-, second-, and third-person methodologies of teaching and learning
- combining critical thinking with experiential feeling
- including the insights of constructive developmental psychology
- including multiple ways of knowing
- weaving together the domains of self, culture, and nurture
- recognizing various types of learners and teachers
- encouraging "shadow work" within learners and teachers, an exploration of the nonrational side of the human self

A truly integrative education engages students in the systematic exploration of the relationship between their studies of the "objective" world and the purpose, meaning, limits, and aspirations of their lives. The greatest divide of all is often between the inner and outer, which no curricular innovation alone can bridge. The healing of this divide is at the heart of education during the college years, rightly understood.

THE NEW SCIENCES AND THE SOCIAL FIELD

Against this background of recent efforts at integrative education, we offer our views, animated by the belief that a philosophy of integrative education cannot be achieved simply by adding up the pedagogical parts, no matter how excellent the parts may be. If integrative learning is to achieve coherence, intentionality, trajectory, and power, it needs a coherent philosophical infrastructure—one that can support, amplify, and multiply the important work already under way and lead to as yet untried innovations. Our thinking about that infrastructure has been heavily influenced by two related sources: the so-called new sciences and a relational approach to meaning and power that centers on what some have called "the social field."

Classical science has had a major impact on how Western culture conceives the nature of the world and the human self, advancing civilization in certain respects but deforming it in others—especially as it has led us to regard ourselves, each other, and the things of the world as objects rather than beings. The "old sciences" have been especially formative in the way we conceive of and practice higher education, profoundly affecting our notions of knowledge, research, analysis, critical thinking, and effectiveness, for better and for worse.

But the new sciences of the 20th century are fundamentally different from those of the classical period, and any re-envisioning of higher education should take seriously what we have learned from them. It is imperative that we look at the higher education for the twenty-first century not through the lenses of Newton and Descartes but of Einstein and Bohr, whose science is not of matter and mechanism but of relationships and dynamic processes. We made extensive use of those lenses in the conversations that led to this book.

In particular, we focused on the primacy of the participating observer whose experiences and relationships form the core of the new sciences. This emphasis on the lived experience of the scientific "observer" links the power of scientific knowing with the feelings we have before a work of art and the compassion we feel for those who suffer, a shift of perspective whose implications are pivotal for higher education. In this view, the relationships and experiences of our lives—and the lives of our students—are not dismissed as irrelevant or inconsequential but are fully granted their own standing as building blocks of reality; they are not secondary qualities or adaptive strategies but primary dimensions of our humanity. In this book, we take these linkages seriously and inquire after their implications for higher education.

The second and related influence in the thinking behind this book derives from a particular kind of experience we can have of each other, one characterized by Martin Buber as an I-Thou relationship.[17] We have all had the experience of a conversation shifting and becoming a deep, free exchange of thoughts and feelings that seems to reach into and beyond the individual participants. Something new emerges, a transcendent communal whole that is greater than the sum of its parts. In such conversations we are caught up for a time in what some call "the social field" generated by the quality of "presence" necessary for true dialogue or community.[18]

Call it what you will, conversations that take place within such a field can, we believe, be particularly generative. They allow us to explore shared concerns selflessly and achieve unexpected insights as our desire to "win" as individuals yields to the desire that the full resources of the community be tapped for the common good. In classrooms, the high points of a course are often exactly those occasions when a discussion takes on this special character. And there are parallel moments in the arts, as when a painting becomes so alive for us that an I-Thou relation is established with it: in that moment we behold the painting in ways that set the experience apart from a more objective or analytic study, mirroring what the new sciences say about the relation of the knower and the known.

Renewing the heart of higher education requires the kind of institutional change that can emerge as academics foster and practice a social capacity of this type. The change we seek within the academy is not one that flows from administrative mandate, but one that arises in the energized space between caring and thoughtful human beings. When personal agendas subside, and genuine interest in the other is established, then a quality of mutual attentiveness emerges that can become the safe harbor for the new and the unexpected that may become a seedbed of educational renewal.

THE AIMS AND LIMITS OF THIS BOOK

Movements for institutional change have always been fueled by significant conversations, a point we develop in considerable detail in Chapter 6. As the San Francisco conference of February 2007 ended, we wondered how we might help its stream of conversation flow stronger, especially around our concern for the philosophical infrastructure of integrative education. In particular, we wondered how colleagues can think and talk together about the elements of that infrastructure—not only at conferences and in books but in the course of doing the everyday work of college and university life—evolving them and integrating them into their ongoing work.

This book is an offering toward that end. As the book gets under way, it is important—just as it is with a good conversation—to be clear about its boundaries and its goals, lest those who consider entering this stream get taken some place they do not want to go.

This is not a book of teaching techniques or programmatic proposals, although it does include stories of practice. Our focus is on exploring the kinds of philosophical questions noted above, to the end of bringing more coherence, and thus more power, to a movement that can sometimes look like an inchoate collection of pedagogical devices. How-to-do-it questions are important in any field of work. But on what premises? and toward what ends? are questions that help create the necessary context for meaningful answers to the how-to question.

Is it true, as Wendell Berry claims, that "universities are *mandated* to make or help to make ... human beings in the fullest sense of those words"? If so, what does that premise mean? And how does acting on that premise pedagogically translate into the "good work and good citizenship" that Berry posits as its "inevitable by-product?" When these questions go unasked and unanswered, a profession can become obsessed with methodology at the expense of its underlying root system and *raison d'etre,* leading to uprooting, distortion, and even malpractice.

This book is an exploration. We have not tried to write a twenty-first century educational version of Thomas Aquinas's *Summa Theologica*; we are nowhere near qualified for that task, and the condition of contemporary culture does not support it. But even though a general field theory of integrative education is nowhere in sight, we believe that this movement—and, indeed, higher education at large—could benefit from more talk about "first and last things." So we offer conversational options regarding starting points and goals, any one of which could open into a deeper probe into the origins, ends, and trajectory of integrative education.

Finally, please note the "reading line" that follows the title and subtitle of this book: "Transforming the Academy Through Collegial Conversation." By focusing on conversation as a tool for institutional renewal, we are adhering to the old Southern folk adage "Dance with the one what brung you!" Most of the gifts higher education has given us have come through good conversation. And both of us—in roles ranging from classroom teacher to community organizer—have experienced the power of conversation to help change challenging realities into promising possibilities. As an exploration, this book is a work in progress, and that progress will continue only as others join in the exploration by coming together in conversation.

While we devote part of this book to a strategy for "renewing the academy" by making more breathing room for integrative education within it, please note that we have no master plan for turning higher education from its current course by commandeering the bridge and creating change from the top down. Higher education has a long historical track record of being impervious to such approaches to change. Instead, we draw on another stream of history, on the story of social movements that have created change from the bottom up. We make a case for conversation itself—focused and disciplined conversation—as a course-changing strategy.

The conversational strategy may not transform the university's infrastructure in the short run. But fundamental change in institutions has always come from planting small communities of vision and practice within those settings; those communities can grow from good conversation; and those conversations can be started by individuals, whether or not they hold positional power. We know this because we have seen it happen.

WHAT LIES AHEAD

In the pages that follow, our call for a wider and deeper conversation about integrative education unfolds through six chapters and a brief conclusion.

We begin with an edited version of Parker Palmer's keynote lecture at the 2007 San Francisco conference. In Chapters 1 and 2, Palmer responds to some typical criticisms of integrative education, addressing the truths that they point to, sometimes offering a critique of the critiques, and suggesting some key dimensions of a philosophy of integrative education as he goes.

Palmer begins with our assumptions about the nature of being (ontology) and knowing (epistemology) that underlie all education, then proceeds to identify questions of teaching-and-learning (pedagogy) and its moral outcomes in the lives of students (ethics). He proposes that the red thread running through all four of these philosophical domains—the thread that more than any other characterizes integrative education—is the concept of community in its many iterations. Community, he argues, is the dimension of reality needed to transform the lingering distortions of Descartes' *cogito, ergo sum* and the myth of objectivism.

In Chapters 3 through 5, Arthur Zajonc takes Palmer's themes and develops them from his own experience as a teacher-scholar. He argues that as educators increasingly focus on basic skills like writing, critical thinking, and numeracy, we too often fail to address issues that are equally central to the life of young adults concerning purpose, core values, and direction in life. As a result we teach and learn in "divided" institutions in which one set of objectives is sanctioned and a second set concerned with the very meaning of education is forgotten.

Zajonc moves from the story of his own divided life as a university student to how, as a professor of physics, he has embraced a view that values experiential and transformative learning as forms of "contemplative knowing." He shows the ways in which our world is richly interconnected and argues that our philosophy of education should reflect that reality. In advancing his case, Zajonc makes equal use of the "new science"—a key paradigm not only of his life and work but of contemporary academic and intellectual life—and his long experience as a college professor.

As Zajonc elaborates on the philosophical infrastructure Palmer has given, he includes not only examples drawn from his own teaching experience but also several short contributions by distinguished colleagues who strive to embody integrative teaching and learning. Each contribution describes a particular effort at realizing one or more aspects of integrative education in the classroom, through community engagement, or via innovative administrative practices. When taken together and read against the backdrop of our text, we believe they can be seen as expressions of a comprehensive, overarching education philosophy that seeks to cultivate the whole human being in community.

We hope that our exploration of an educational philosophy, seen together with these examples of its initial expression, will stimulate our colleagues in higher education to generate new pedagogical initiatives to fill the gaps, contributing to a renewal of the educational enterprise.

Having explored some of the all-important "first and last things" of integrative education, with examples, we turn in Chapter 6 to an in-depth exploration of a "conversational strategy" for educational reform. This is a strategy familiar to community organizers—whose ways of thinking and acting may not be well-known in the academy—and is, we believe, key to planting seeds of change on campus.

Conversations that cultivate the philosophical ground explored in the first five chapters can, we believe, till the soil in which these seeds of change are planted. And when the tillers of the soil have made the investment that cultivation requires and gained the confidence that working together engenders, it is no great leap for them to become the active planters of the seeds of pedagogical experimentation. This has already begun to happen, and the exemplars we include are evidence of its power.

In order for new seeds to take root and sprout, the support of academic administrators and trustees will be invaluable. But the roots of deep and lasting change in higher education lie, we believe, with small groups of faculty, student life administrators, other staff, and students, creating the kind of innovations on which progress in every field depends—the ones that come not from a well-financed lab but from a garage behind someone's house. So Chapter 6 offers guidance for the practice of deep speaking and listening on which good conversation depends and proposes a conversational trajectory that starts with stories, moves into theory, and emerges in action.

Finally, in wide-ranging appendices compiled by Megan Scribner, a key conversation partner who helped us create this book, we offer an annotated list of integrative education programs and projects going on around the country. Each in its own way attempts to bring the ideal of educating the whole student into concrete expression both inside and outside the classroom—and each bears witness to the fact that it can be done. These appendices are *not* a comprehensive survey of all the experimentation going on in higher education today; they primarily consist of projects we learned about via the 2007 conference. But even this limited listing proves that an integrated approach to the aims of education can find diverse practical expressions: *E pluribus unum!*

The responsibilities of our colleges and universities are immense, especially when we consider the complexity and fragility of today's world economically, politically, socially, and environmentally. Every resource of our humanity, as individuals and as communities, will be needed if we are to safely navigate the shoals of the future. Clearly, higher education is one of the institutions that must rise to that challenge.

In the face of that enormous task, we offer this small book and make a modest proposal. Sit down with at least one or two other people who have stakes in higher education and create the conditions in which you can express authentic feelings, think creative thoughts, and speak your truth to each other's mind and heart. In our own lives as teachers, the authors of this book have learned that when we speak and listen truly and well with colleagues, we can begin to weave a new imagination for higher education out of our shared experiences—and that our communal imagination can evolve into new ways of teaching and learning.

Collectively, as students, teachers, and administrators, we have the wisdom and experience we need to meet the challenges of the century ahead—if we are brave enough to name what we care about, share what we know, and take the risks that transformation always requires.

Chapter 1

Toward a Philosophy of Integrative Education

Parker J. Palmer

Those of us who advocate for integrative higher education in the opening years of the twenty-first century stand in a long line of would-be reformers. An on-again, off-again movement to make America's approach to higher education more multidimensional has been at work since before there was a United States.

In 1774, representatives from Maryland and Virginia negotiated a treaty with the Indians of the Six Nations, who were then invited to send their boys to the college of William and Mary, founded in 1693. The tribal elders declined that offer with the following words:

> We know that you highly esteem the kind of learning taught in those Colleges, and that the Maintenance of our young Men, while with you, would be very expensive to you. We are

convinced that you mean to do us Good by your Proposal; and we thank you heartily. But you, who are wise must know that different Nations have different Conceptions of things and you will therefore not take it amiss, if our ideas of this kind of Education happen not to be the same as yours. We have had some Experience of it. Several of our young People were formerly brought up at the Colleges of the Northern Provinces: they were instructed in all your Sciences; but, when they came back to us, they were bad Runners, ignorant of every means of living in the woods … neither fit for Hunters, Warriors, nor Counsellors, they were totally good for nothing.

We are, however, not the less oblig'd by your kind offer, tho' we decline accepting it; and, to show our grateful Sense of it, if the Gentlemen of Virginia will send us a Dozen of their Sons, we will take Care of their Education, instruct them in all we know, and make Men of them.[1]

Here we are, two and a half centuries later, wanting the same thing these tribal elders wanted, in principle if not in detail: an education that embraces every dimension of what it means to be human, that honors the varieties of human experience, looks at us and our world through a variety of cultural lenses, and educates our young people in ways that enable them to face the challenges of our time.

The institution of higher education is notoriously slow to change. But many individuals within the institution have kept the vision of an integrative practice alive in their hearts—using *heart* in its original sense, not just as the seat of the emotions but as that core place in the human self where all our capacities converge: intellect, senses, emotions, imagination, intuition, will, spirit, and soul.

There are good and bad reasons for the slow pace of institutional change. One of an institution's key functions is to conserve the best of the past over time, serving as a collective memory bank to protect us against historical amnesia, cultural erosion, and the seductions of the merely new. For this we can be grateful. But institutions sometimes cling to their routines out of fear of change and under

THE HEART OF HIGHER EDUCATION

the cover of the arrogance of power: when you are the only game in town, you do not need to listen to your critics.

If higher education is to keep evolving toward its full potential, it needs people who are so devoted to the educational enterprise that they have a lover's quarrel with the institution whenever they see it fall short of that potential—and are willing to translate that quarrel into positive action. We need to uncover and empower the heart of higher education in those faculty, administrators, students, alumni, and trustees who have a vision for reclaiming the unrealized potentials in the human and historical DNA that gave rise to academic life.

MODES OF KNOWING

At the heart of any serious approach to educational reform is a set of questions about the core functions of the university: knowing, teaching, and learning. Advocates for integrative education take facts and rationality seriously; the failure to do so would betray our DNA. But we also seek forms of knowing, teaching, and learning that offer more nourishment than the thin soup served up when data and logic are the only ingredients. In our complex and demanding worlds—inner *and* outer worlds—the human species cannot survive, let alone thrive, on a diet like that.

I have long been impressed by the fact that science itself—great science, original science, the science on which so much of modern culture is built—depends on our subtle faculties as much as it does on objective data and logical analysis. It depends on bodily knowledge, intuition, imagination, and aesthetic sensibility, as you can learn from any mathematician who has been led to a proof by its "elegance." The hard sciences are full-body sports, enterprises that depend on experiential immersion in the phenomena and the process. To quote that classic of children's literature *The Wind in the Willows*, the greatest of scientists have always thrived on "messing about in boats."[2]

I find it helpful from time to time to reread Michael Polanyi's fifty-year-old classic, *Personal Knowledge*.[3] Polanyi, a physical chemist and philosopher of science, argues that our scientific

Toward a Philosophy of Integrative Education

knowledge is dependent on us being in the world as whole persons, that if we did not have bodies and selves that "indwell" the physical phenomena of the world in an altogether inarticulate way, we could not know any of what we know at an articulate conceptual, logical, empirical level. Our *explicit* knowing depends, argues Polanyi, on a vast subterranean layer of *tacit* human knowing, and we will be arrogant about the hegemony of science until we learn to honor its wordless underground foundations. Reading Polanyi made me realize that a student who says, "I know what I mean but I don't know how to say it," is not *necessarily* blowing smoke!

When we honor the hidden aquifer that feeds human knowing, we are more likely to develop a capacity for awe, wonder, and humility that deepens rather than diminishes our knowledge. And we are less likely to develop the kind of hubris about our knowledge that haunts the world today. So much of the violence our culture practices at home and exports abroad is rooted in an arrogance that says, "We know best, and we are ready to enforce what we know politically, culturally, economically, militarily." In contrast, a mode of knowing steeped in awe, wonder, and humility is a mode of knowing that can serve the human cause, which is the whole point of integrative education.

Human knowing, rightly understood, has paradoxical roots—mind and heart, hard data and soft intuition, individual insight and communal sifting and winnowing—the roots novelist Vladimir Nabokov pointed to when he told his Cornell University students that they must do their work "with the passion of the scientist and precision of the poet."[4] Integrative education aims to "think the world together" rather than "think it apart," to know the world in a way that empowers educated people to act on behalf of wholeness rather than fragmentation.

The philosophical infrastructure of integrative education is a very large topic. I will try to bring it down to scale by framing these two opening chapters as "a dialogue with the critics," an encounter with five archetypal criticisms of integrative education that I have heard or intuited over the years. As I look back on my own work in higher education, I am clear that I have learned more from my critics than from my fans. Criticism awakens me at three o'clock in the morning, compelling me to chew on things in a way I never do when people tell me that I got something right.

There is another reason I want to bring the critics into this conversation up front. In my judgment, one of the saddest and most self-contradictory features of academic culture is the way it tends to run away from criticism. Academic culture celebrates "critical thinking," often elevating that capacity to its number-one goal for students. But academic culture is sometimes dominated by orthodoxy as profoundly as any church I know. If a mode of knowing, a pedagogy, a life experience, or social perspective is not regarded as kosher in the academy, it too often does not get a fair hearing. So if we are serious about integrative education, we must give a fair hearing to those who disagree with us. As we do so, we have a chance to model and help restore one of the academy's highest norms when it comes to good inquiry: engaging contradictory ideas in creative conflict.

CRITIQUE 1: WEAK PHILOSOPHICAL FOUNDATIONS

In this chapter and the next, I want to explore five critiques of integrative education. Some of them have been made explicitly, while others I regard as the unspoken and underlying reasons why the academy has often resisted an integrative approach to its mission. The first critique—which has four subsections and will occupy the rest of this chapter—is that integrative education is a grab bag of techniques that have no philosophical underpinnings, coherence, or power, that it is merely an assortment of pedagogies like service learning, action research, and small-group process, behind which there is no deep-rooted or defensible educational philosophy.

Up to a point, the critics are right—if they weren't, there would be little need for this book! The integrative education movement has been obsessed with questions of technique. But the weakness

Toward a Philosophy of Integrative Education

of the philosophical case for integrative education is not because none can be mounted. It is because many of us have not done our homework on these issues in a way that allows us to engage our critics in a constructive dialogue—hampered, perhaps, by a sense of having a "country cousin" relationship to our city cousins in the academy who embrace and are emboldened by the power of academic orthodoxy.

We cannot advance this movement by remaining on the margins and tinkering with methodology. We need to draw on the deep and rich philosophical resources that are readily available to us, that are found at the heart of the classic traditions that gave rise to higher education. The subtle faculties on which great science depends—including nonrational forms of intelligence such as bodily knowing, relationality, intuition, and emotion—deserve the most rational defense we can give them. Our challenge is to become more conversant with these things and more articulate about them, in dialogue with the critics.

As we move in that direction, two interesting ironies are worth noting. One is that in the university—where issues in the philosophy of education ought to be regular topics of discussion—the discussion, as everyone knows, is much more likely to be about who gets on-campus parking or the bigger slice of the credit-hour pie. Advocates of integrative education can serve the general renewal of academic culture well by putting subjects of more fundamental importance into play.

The second irony is this: the philosophical foundations of conventional pedagogy are so weak that no one even tries to mount a philosophical defense of them. For example, it is widely understood that the division of intellectual labor represented by discipline-bound academic departments is not the most illuminating way to gain knowledge of a complex world, which is why interdisciplinary studies are at the growing edge of the evolution of learning. But most teaching continues to occur within disciplinary silos, not because it is philosophically defensible but simply because that is how things have always been done. So if the critics who represent academic orthodoxy want a conversation about philosophical foundations, they face challenges of their own. We need a genuine dialogue in which the partners help each other move past their own limitations for the sake of the larger enterprise.

I want to offer a few notes toward that possibility under the four philosophical rubrics of ontology, epistemology, pedagogy, and ethics, which I regard as foundational to the educational enterprise at large, including integrative education. These four as I understand them are woven together by the concept of "community," not merely as a sociological phenomenon but as an *ontological reality*, an *epistemological necessity*, a *pedagogical asset*, and an *ethical corrective*. Of course, in the brief span of a chapter, I cannot begin to do justice to questions that philosophers have grappled with for centuries. I hope simply to help make these questions part of the conversation, knowing that Arthur Zajonc will address them in more depth later in this book.

An Ontological Reality

Ian Barbour, the distinguished philosopher of science, offers a quick and helpful three-stage summary of the complex history of ontology, the nature of being and how we perceive it, at least in Western civilization. In the medieval era, says Barbour, we viewed reality as mental and material "substance" or "stuff." "In the Newtonian era our image of reality became atomistic, positing separate particles, rather than substances, to be the basic nature of reality."[5]

Philosophical ideas sometimes have a trickle-down effect. The image of atoms colliding in the void as the building blocks of reality morphed into a way of thinking that had massive societal implications. In the Western world, it got translated (with the help of social Darwinism) into an atomistic notion of the self and a competitive "survival of the fittest" concept of human relations. That view, in turn, helped shape an educational system premised on the notion that knowledge consists of collecting atomistic facts about an atomistic reality, facts to be delivered by individuals who know them to others who do not in a system where learners compete with each other for scarce rewards.

25

But today, in stage three of Barbour's brief history of ontology, the atomistic view of being is starting to lose its grip on our cultural imagination:

> Nature is understood now to be relational, ecological, and interdependent. Reality is constituted by events and relationships rather than separate substances or separate particles. We are now compelled to see nature as "a historical community of interdependent beings."[6]

Physicist Henry Stapp says it is no longer possible even to think of the atom as a discrete entity: "an elementary particle is not an independently existing, unanalyzable entity. It is, in essence, a set of relationships that reach outward to other things."[7]

This relational ontology, rooted in reflections on the findings of particle physics, is just beginning to permeate our thought patterns, self-understandings, and ways of being in the world—though we still have a long way to go in overcoming our habit of thinking of reality as "atoms colliding in the void," an image that can all too accurately describe the felt experience of contemporary life. The good news is that seeing the cosmos as "a historical community of interdependent beings" has opened the way to systems theory in institutional life; to ecology and deep ecology in our study of nature; to depth and Gestalt psychology as we explore our inner landscapes; to integrative forms of teaching and learning that resemble an interactive and interdependent community that transcends "nature red in tooth and claw."

Much depends on the assumptions we make about the nature of being, the nature of the reality in which we are embedded that is also embedded in us. Those of us who advocate integrative education can make a strong case that ours is an approach to teaching and learning faithful to new understandings of how the cosmos is constituted. Helping students come to terms with reality is a fundamental aim of higher education, an unattainable goal when the unexamined foundations of education, the "hidden curriculum," are atomistic and competitive rather than interconnected and communal.

An Epistemological Necessity

Integrative education begins with the premise that we are embedded in a communal reality and then proceeds to an epistemological assertion: we cannot know this communal reality truly and well unless we ourselves are consciously and actively in community with it as knowers.

Of course, whether we know it or not, like it or not, honor it or not, we are in community with reality. We are communal creatures from the subatomic level, through our conscious and unconscious inner lives, to the social relationships and institutional arrangements that constitute our external worlds. The only question is whether we will embrace that fact and, in the case of education, re-vision our understanding of what it means to know, teach, and learn.

Contrary to the objectivist myth that has dominated higher education, the knower cannot be separated from the known for the sake of so-called objectivity. Given what we now understand about the mutually influential relationship of the knower and the known, objectivism is no longer a viable way to frame knowing, teaching, or learning, or the true meaning of objectivity, for that matter. Those of us who advocate for integrative education need to make this point foundational to our efforts.

I believe in objectivity, which is to say that I believe in a model of knowing that goes beyond truth claims made by individuals on merely subjective grounds. Objectivity, rightly understood, emerges from testing what we *think* we know in the context of a community of inquiry guided by shared principles and practices. But I also believe that there is no way to eliminate human subjectivity from human knowing—after all, another name for science's way of testing validity in community is "inter-subjective verifiability." Not only is eliminating subjectivity impossible but, as Polanyi argues in *Personal Knowledge*, we would know hardly anything were it not for the subjective foundations of knowing, including bodily knowing.[8]

There is a story from the heart of great science that makes the point as well as any I know. Nobel Prize–winning geneticist Barbara McClintock was the first to uncover the mysteries of genetic transposition, doing so at a time when we lacked the instruments to observe the phenomena directly. She did it through a process rooted partly in what one can only call "mysticism." When she died at age ninety, McClintock was eulogized by a distinguished colleague as "someone who understands where the mysteries lie" rather than "someone who mystifies," a powerful description of a sensibility often found at the heart of great science.[9]

McClintock's work was chronicled in a book by Evelyn Fox Keller, professor of history and philosophy at the Massachusetts Institute of Technology. Keller asked McClintock, in effect, "What's the secret of your great science?" and summarizes her answer with these words:

> Over and over again she tells us one must have the time to look, the patience to "hear what the material has to say to you," the openness to "let it come to you." Above all, one must have "a feeling for the organism."[10]

When pressed for her secret, this keen observer with a finely tuned logical mind, the winner of a Nobel Prize, speaks of the maize plants that were her primary experimental materials not as objects but as beings. She understood that we can know a relational reality only by being in relation to it—not keeping our distance, as in the objectivist mythology, but moving close and leaning in, then testing what we think we know against the standards of evidence and logic in the context of the scientific community. McClintock, says one writer, "gained valuable knowledge by empathizing with her corn plants, submerging herself in their world and dissolving the boundary between object and observer."[11] Biographer Keller sums up McClintock's genius—and the genius of all integrative knowing—in a single luminous sentence: McClintock, in her relation to ears of corn, achieved "the highest form of love, love that allows for intimacy without the annihilation of difference."[12] When I read that, I thought, "Here's someone who had the kind of relationship with ears of corn that I yearn to have with other people!"

At bottom, knowing and loving significantly overlap each other: there are passions of the mind that are almost indistinguishable from passions of the heart in the energy they generate. That is why the eleventh-century theologian St. Simeon described the deepest form of human knowing as the result of thinking with "the mind descended into the heart."

A Pedagogical Asset

The ontology and epistemology I have explored here offer scant comfort to any pedagogy that involves dumping factoids into the "empty vessel" of the student's head. Instead, they lead to a pedagogy of carefully crafted relationships of student to teacher, student to student, and teacher to student to subject. A relational ontology and epistemology can take us in no other pedagogical direction than this. We must get past the inertia and the fear of experimentation that has kept too much of academic culture frozen in pedagogical practices that are out of phase with what we now understand about the nature of reality and the dynamics of knowing.

This does not rule out lecturing, because there are ways of lecturing that can create or help community, for example, in the way a well-staged theatrical drama does. But a pedagogy shaped by relational principles and practices requires a virtue not always found in university classrooms: hospitality. Learning spaces need to be hospitable spaces not merely because kindness is a good idea but because real education requires rigor. In a counterintuitive way, hospitality supports rigor by supporting community, and the proof can be found in everyday classroom experience.

Pedagogical rigor requires more than a professor doing a rigorous solo act, which can feel more like *rigor mortis* from where the student sits. A classroom becomes rigorous when a student is able to raise his or her hand and say, "I disagree with what you just said, professor." Or, at even greater personal risk, "I disagree with what my friend in the second row just said." Or, pulling out all the stops, "Excuse me, I don't understand anything that's been said in here for the past two weeks. Could someone please explain?"

Admitting ignorance and encountering diverse viewpoints on facts and interpretations require us to clarify our assertions, explain ourselves at deeper levels and perhaps, *mirabile dictu,* even change our minds. Professors who encourage student behaviors such as these invite true intellectual rigor, the kind that emerges from a community of inquiry and is far more educational than a nonstop diet of "rigorous" lectures. From where the students sit, these behaviors are also riskier than keeping one's head down and taking notes. That kind of behavior is not going to happen in a class that lacks hospitality, a class where people feel too threatened to say anything that might get them crosswise with the professor or other students.

Academic culture has long made a false distinction between the "hard" virtues of scholarship and the "soft" virtues of community, putting the first in the hands of the faculty and the second in the hands of the office of student life. In truth, the soft virtues and the hard virtues go hand in hand when it comes to good pedagogy. I did my doctoral work at the University of California at Berkeley. Occasionally, when we were not listening to lectures, we were in seminars where people played intellectual hardball. Under those circumstances, it was rare to hear an honest open question, to say nothing of an admission of ignorance. The questions, for the most part, were designed to let the professor know that the questioner knew what the professor wanted to hear. Rigor is not to be confused with playing hardball, which usually is a form of gaming that is essentially anti-intellectual, played to score points rather than seek understanding.

Today, the integrative education movement has a sizeable catalogue of methods of teaching and learning that support the idea of a "learning community." From Socrates with his devotion to dialogical inquiry, to late twentieth-century innovations such as "learning communities" and service learning, the history of education is dotted with alternatives to the kind of information dumping that was bred by the myth of objectivism. The great need of the integrative education movement is not for new and better techniques but for an ongoing exploration of the philosophical foundations of this movement—from which we can responsibly challenge the conventional pedagogy, hone and deepen the methods in our current catalogue, and invent new methods that honor our fundamental principles.

An Ethical Corrective

Every epistemology, or way of knowing, as implemented in a pedagogy, or way of teaching and learning, tends to become an ethic, or way of living. This final foundation stone in the infrastructure of integrative education points to a critical fact: integrative forms of teaching and learning support a kind of ethical thinking and action that an objectivist education does not.

An objectivist epistemology is based on the myth that we must hold the world at arm's length in order to know it purely, untainted by subjectivity, then transmit what we know in ways that keep us and our students distanced from that world. It stands to reason that this form of education would breed "educated" people whose knowledge of the world is so abstract that they cannot engage the world morally: disengaged forms of learning are likely to lead learners toward disengaged lives. What students learn about poverty from reading texts is almost always less compelling than what they would have learned by doing that reading while volunteering in a community where the sights, sounds, and smells of poverty are inescapable elements of the educational experience. The kind of "distance education" that objectivism breeds lays the ground for lives lived at a distance from the suffering of the world.

As a student, I learned about the Holocaust from historians who presented the facts and figures in an academically antiseptic way, at objectivist arm's length. My teachers never invited Holocaust survivors to come to class and tell their stories. They never showed us films of human beings lined up on the edge of ditches and shot from behind by grinning soldiers, of skeletal survivors of the death camps being freed by Allied troops, of bodies piled up like cordwood around the camp grounds. I knew the facts and figures. But they had been taught to me in such a dispassionate manner that I held my knowledge of these horrors at great distance from my life, held it as if these things had happened to some other species on some other planet.

Only later did I begin to understand that the community in which I had grown up—a community where "people like them" were geographically separated from "people like us"—was shaped by systematic real estate practices rooted in the same forces of darkness that drove the Holocaust. On a more personal level, only later did I begin to understand that I have within myself a certain "fascism of the heart" that would "kill off" anyone who threatens my cherished world view—not with a gas chamber, but with a mental or verbal dismissal that renders that person irrelevant to my life.

Not until I appropriated the history of the Holocaust as a lens through which to scrutinize my own life story did I begin to lay the foundations for my own moral response to such evil. This is something I should have been given help doing in the course of my education. Lacking that dimension, the phrase "educated person" becomes hollow. We need to understand why a large percentage of the people who oversaw the murder of six million Jews had doctoral degrees from some of the "great" universities of the era. We need to understand how integrative forms of teaching and learning can mitigate against educational travesties and tragedies such as this.

Every epistemology—rooted (as all of them are) in a particular ontology, and manifesting (as all of them do) in a particular pedagogy—has an impact on the ethical formation of learners. Epistemology becomes operational in students' lives not through overt conversation or explicit knowing but through modes of teaching and learning that tacitly form or deform learners in a particular way of relating to the world. An integrative pedagogy is more likely to lead to moral engagement because it engages more of the learner's self and teaches by means of engagement: the curriculum *and* the "hidden curriculum" embedded in such a pedagogy support a way of knowing that involves much if not all of the whole self in learning about the world.

The "trickle-down" traced in this chapter—from ontology through epistemology through pedagogy to ethics—is something that we who care about integrative education must talk more about, with each other and with the critics. Doing so would help us consolidate the strong philosophical underpinnings of integrative education and help this movement become more credible, more effective, and more inventive.

Chapter 2

When Philosophy Is Put into Practice

Parker J. Palmer

Having responded to a series of issues related to the first critique of integrative education—that it lacks clear and compelling philosophical foundations—I want to explore a series of concerns that arise when we try to teach in a way consistent with its premises and goals. The challenges of implementing integrative education in the classroom—especially those that make demands on the teacher for which we may be unprepared—deserve our close attention lest we abandon our philosophical commitments when faced with classroom realities.

CRITIQUE 2: INTEGRATIVE EDUCATION IS TOO MESSY

The second critique that advocates of integrative teaching and learning must address is that this pedagogy is too "messy" to qualify as higher learning. Responding to this critique will not divert us from exploring the philosophy of integrative education. Instead, as I hope to show, it will take us deeper into the ethical issues touched on in Chapter 1.

The kind of knowledge most valued in the academy is that which can be dealt with in a rational, linear, and controlled manner; words such as those define the comfort zone in academic culture. But when it comes to questions involving relational knowledge, bodily knowledge, intuitive knowledge, or emotional knowledge, more than a few academics draw a line they are loathe cross—sometimes because they feel unqualified to deal with knowledge of that sort, sometimes because they do not regard it as credible knowledge in the first place.

There is considerable emotional energy behind this critique. But it is rarely made explicit and tends to emerge indirectly, as when the critics argue against certain integrative pedagogies—such as a course that forgoes a page-by-page forced march through basic texts in favor of some degree of hands-on engagement with the subject—on the grounds that they do not allow us to "cover the field" in a systematic way, tracking a stepwise accumulation of knowledge and measuring student progress "objectively" via standardized tests.

As those who have done it know, an integrative approach to teaching and learning *can* get messy. But it gets no messier than life itself and, done well, can help bring order to chaotic raw experience, as is the case with any well-crafted cycle of action and reflection. The real question is whether we want higher education to be about life.

In answer to the inevitable "What else is there?" a case can be made that too much of higher education deals with something else: an engagement with what the critics say about a poem, not with what the poem evokes from my experience; an engagement with social science artifacts that have currency in professional journals, not with lived social facts. That kind of education can yield measurable and gradable outcomes that lead to a college degree and perhaps, as the student advances, a career in an academic guild. But that kind of education does not prepare students well for the world beyond the academy.

In 1969, I left Berkeley with a PhD in sociology to become a community organizer in the Washington, D.C., area. I knew many sociological artifacts about American society, as in "the average American family has 1.86 children" (an updated number, based on the 2000 U.S. Census). Of course, as I went about my organizing tasks in the Takoma Park–East Silver Spring neighborhood, I never met such a family; the intellectual habits that lead to statistics like that, which served me well in graduate school and would have continued to serve me well had I become a professor of sociology, were not helpful to me as I tried to engage the world in three dimensions and living color as a community organizer. Knowledge that works well in academic journals does not necessarily work so well on the streets.

I am not suggesting that none of my Berkeley education was serviceable once I left grad school. For example, C. Wright Mills's notion of "the sociological imagination" as a way of seeing and being in the world was extraordinarily helpful to me. But that little word *imagination* tells a big story, for it is not a word to be found in the objectivist vocabulary. As an organizer, I had to unlearn a lot of objectivist intellectual habits. Since graduates in many fields face the same steep learning curve—some of which, of course, is necessary and desirable, since life demands that we become perpetual learners—why not give students some experience with *in situ* self-education before we release them into the wild, the kind of experience that is part and parcel of integrative pedagogies?

Academic culture includes what some have called a "purity obsession," a commitment to keeping our work as orderly as possible, an obsession that has been a source of much societal distress. Think, for example, of the accountants who learned orderly bookkeeping procedures from orderly textbooks in orderly business school

When Philosophy Is Put into Practice

classes and then went to work at very messy places like Enron where they helped destroy a chunk of the global economy and rob hundreds of thousands of individuals of a decent retirement in the process. There are accountants who did exactly that, not because they were dishonest, but because their orderly education did not prepare them to deal with real-world convolutions and subterfuges. They took the only formulas they knew, the ones at the back of the book, and applied them to problems where formulaic thinking concealed rather than revealed the truth, with catastrophic results.

Now raise the moral stakes even higher and consider the complicity of German higher education in the Holocaust. Here, the purity obsession that forbade "real scholars" from engaging with the messy affairs of the world made German higher education a partner to one of the most massive evils in human history. In *Hitler's Death Camps,* by Konnilyn G. Feig, there is a passage that could be engraved across the arched entryway to every university, posted on the door of every classroom, handed out with every course syllabus, and tacked on the bulletin board over every professor's desk:

> We have identified certain "civilizing" aspects of the modern
> world—music, art, a sense of family, love, appreciation of
> beauty, intellect, education .... [But] after Auschwitz we must
> realize that being a killer, a family man, and a lover of
> Beethoven are not contradictions. The killers did not belong to
> a gutter society of misfits, nor could they be dismissed as just a
> collection of rabble. They were scholars, artists, lawyers,
> theologians and aristocrats.[1]

If higher education cannot deal with the messiness of real life, educated people will not be prepared to use their knowledge amid the complexities and cruelties that constantly threaten to undo civilization. And they clearly will not know how to use their knowledge with wisdom, compassion, and love. Love itself is messy, risky, and sometimes very dangerous. As Dostoevsky said, "Love in action is a harsh and dreadful thing"[2]—just ask the ghosts of the brave souls who rescued Jews from the Holocaust, often at the expense of their own lives. If higher education does not help people learn how and why to take the risks of love, its moral contributions to the world will fall far short of its potential.

And yet, even as we rebut the "messiness" critique, we need to take it to heart. There are, in fact, ways of implementing integrative education that are rightly rejected by the academy because of pedagogical messiness. Integrative education at its best will always be an adventuresome, exploratory, and discovery-oriented form of learning that will never accommodate itself to the foregone conclusions and predictable outcomes on which standardized tests are built. But for that very reason, integrative forms of teaching and learning must have clear intentionality and trajectory, employing pedagogical designs that will take us and our students somewhere worth going.

Our pedagogies must have the power and precision to clarify some of the world's messiness and help students find their way through it rather than multiplying the mess and leaving students more lost. For example, accountants should be thrown into simulations of Enron-type messes while they are still in school and taught to identify anomalies and unravel the kinds of problems that are not named in the text or solved at the back of the book. But they should be thrown in only after they have been taught how to keep their heads above water in dangerous currents, like a kayaker going down a whitewater river through Class 6 rapids.

Doing integrative education well depends on our capacity to hold a paradox: we must open free space for the unpredictable *and* enforce an educative order. In contrast to a top-down delivery of information that leaves the teacher in control, integrative pedagogies involve a communal exchange that is fluid, complex, and confusing. Teachers who use these methods must be able to think on their feet in order to help students learn to do the same. Into that complex flow of communal exploration, teachers must inject intentionality by teaching information, skills, and disciplines that can keep the exploration headed toward a destination worth achieving—an educational outcome that may well require meandering down side roads and into dead ends, even getting lost, but without getting stuck in such places.

As a practitioner of integrative education, I have sometimes been guilty of loosing students to meander without intent. Maintaining intentionality and trajectory in the midst of real-world messiness is demanding, far more demanding than standing at the edge of the wilderness and giving the expeditionary team a lecture about what they might find in there. The only way to learn that art—the art of helping students negotiate the world's complexities, clarifying the mess rather than mucking it up—is for teachers to wrestle with pedagogical principles and practices, individually and as colleagues, with at least the same dedication they ask of students who are trying to learn demanding subjects.

Doing so requires collegial action, from shared discourse about pedagogy to shared support for pedagogical risk taking, topics we explore in Chapter 6. This kind of collegiality is not easily achieved, but neither is it impossible. The faculty I know who have invested themselves in such relationships report better learning outcomes for students and, equally important, new energy for their own academic lives.

CRITIQUE 3: EMOTIONS HAVE NO PLACE IN THE CLASSROOM

The third critique of integrative education is a subset of the second, but it is so common and can be so crippling that it deserves separate treatment, and responding to it will take us deeper into the epistemological issues raised in Chapter 1. The critique is this: methods of integrative education ranging from service learning to working in teams to role playing and journal keeping are capable of evoking strong emotions, but emotions do not belong in the classroom, which should be reserved for teaching the facts and developing the cognitive skills to assess them.

I sometimes hear faculty put this critique in words like these: "I'm not a therapist so don't ask me to act like one." Despite its rhetorical excess, that assertion makes an important point. As a professor, there are places I am not equipped to go with my students. So I must be clear about my limits—clear with myself and with my students. If I invite students to journal about certain topic-related experiences, and I am going to read those journals, I must put boundaries around what they are to submit to me, informing them in advance that I would be guilty of malpractice if I tried to practice therapy. If I get in over my head with a student who does not understand these boundaries, I must partner with people in student affairs who know their way around this territory.

The claim that emotions have no place in the classroom raises serious issues. The problem is that no matter how much we may want to factor them out, emotions will never disappear from the classroom. Wherever two or three are gathered, feelings will be generated—and those feelings will work for or against the aims of education. Show me a classroom "devoid of feelings" and I will show you a classroom in which feelings have been driven underground, where they will do more harm than good to the educational process.

Academic culture needs to embrace the simple fact that cognition, which is our business, is intimately linked to affect, no matter how much we think emotions are not our business. As neuroscientists such as Candace Pert have told us, thinking is not done solely by the *brain*, an organ housed in the cranium.[3] Thinking is done by the *mind,* which is not an organ but a process that is distributed throughout the body and draws on every faculty we have.

Of course, long before recent breakthroughs in neurological science, we had access to the insights of scholars like Sheila Tobias who told us why girls and women, once upon a time, failed so miserably at mathematics.[4] It is not because the female brain is structured in such a way as to make computation difficult, which was the dominant and sexist theory a few short decades ago. Rather, it is because girls were told from a very young age that their gender cannot do math, so they walked into math and science classrooms paralyzed by an emotion called fear. Tobias and her colleagues told us that if we could free the mind from fear's paralysis, females would succeed at math—and because some educators took them seriously, we now know that they were right. Understanding the impact of fear on learning, and weaving that understanding into pedagogical practice, has eliminated gender differences in success at mathematics.

So when I hear faculty dismiss the affective dimension of teaching and learning as "touchy-feely stuff," I have to conclude that they are projecting their personal discomfort with emotions rather than making a statement about the real world. Put-downs like that, applied to pedagogies that deal thoughtfully with the learner's emotions, are irresponsible dismissals of a fundamental pedagogical need and responsibility, to say nothing of the simple facts. When educators have the wit and the will to meet that need, the real-world results are impressive. As everyone should know by now, many women are making significant contributions and very good money at work that requires high levels of functioning in mathematics. If that is the outcome of "touchy-feely" pedagogies, we need a lot more of the same.

There is a pair of tragicomic ironies embedded in academic resistance to taking seriously the connection between feeling and thinking. Academics who want to factor out "subjective emotions" in favor of data-based "objective knowledge" will, at the same time, blithely ignore fifty years of research about the importance of attending to the emotions if we want to liberate the mind. I do not think it unfair to say that such people are "pedagogical fundamentalists" who prooftext the research the way Biblical fundamentalists prooftext the Bible, honoring whatever supports their biases and ignoring the rest.

The paired irony is that these academics ignore all the research-based knowledge we have on the role of emotions in learning largely because embracing the implications of that knowledge would take *them* out of *their* emotional comfort zones! It is enough to make one's head spin. But we who advocate for integrative education ought to be spinning our heads in public, weaving a sound defense for attending to the heart-mind connection, making it more difficult for orthodox academics to be dismissive of brain science, pedagogical reality, and simple common sense.

CRITIQUE 4: RESISTANCE TO COMMUNITY

This fourth critique, like the others considered in this chapter, goes largely unspoken in academic culture, but it creates an undertow that needs to be named. And like the others, this one takes us deeper into a philosophical issue that runs through Chapter 1: the red thread called "community" that runs through every level of integrative education.

Integrative education often requires us to work collaboratively with others, which makes the approach challenging for academics who subscribe to Greta Garbo's signature line, "I vant to be alone." If they were to speak their minds, I believe they would say something like this: "I got into this business for the solitude it offers me to do my work, by which I mean not teaching but my research."

Clearly, there is a place for hermits under the "big umbrella" of university life. Important parts of the intellectual life require solitude and quietude. But integrative teaching and learning suffer when academic culture fails to reward and sometimes even discourages people for forging creative partnerships. I have talked with a number of second-career professors who teach in business schools after spending years in business, asking, "What kinds of culture shock have you experienced in moving from one world to another?" Their response almost always runs along these lines: "In the business world, I couldn't be in my office for three minutes before someone was knocking on the door saying, 'I need help solving this problem.' But in the university, I can sit in my office all day long and no one ever comes calling. I miss the collegiality. I find I'm not thinking fresh thoughts as often as I did in business."

This phenomenon, which I call the privatization of the professoriate, is dysfunctional for individuals and institutions in the world of education. No matter how you slice it, the basic mission of the academy—knowing, teaching, and learning—is, at bottom, communal. That mission cannot be pursued successfully in the absence of cultural support for community.

One of the most important stories I know in support of that claim involves Uri Treisman, who was, at the time, a professor of

When Philosophy Is Put into Practice

mathematics at the University of California at Berkeley.[5] Treisman was distressed by a disparity that many had observed but few had bothered to think deeply about: his African American students were failing math, his Caucasian students were somewhere in the middle, and his Asian American students were doing well.

Like Sheila Tobias, Treisman was unwilling to accept conventional (in this case racist) explanations of these facts, so he studied them with care. What he found was fascinating but simple. If he took a snapshot of how much math any of his students had learned just before they walked out of a class session, the picture would look the same for all three groups: "I understand a little bit of what I just heard, but not much."

The differences kicked in once his students got out the door. The Asian American students went more or less directly to the coffee shop where they sat down and untangled the mysteries of math with one another. Among the Caucasian students, some got together this way and some did not. But the African American students in that time and place belonged to a subculture in which talking with peers about academic matters was not acceptable, so they lacked communal support for learning.

Treisman created a program to help his African American students and others at risk of failure become comfortable doing what his Asian American students were doing for themselves. In relatively short order, he radically reduced racial disparities in success at math, providing a model that others have used with similar results. For this he won a coveted MacArthur Genius Award, and that tells us something we need to remember: as educators, we can be so resistant to secrets hidden in plain sight that *genius* means things like remembering that students can learn from each other.

Our resistance to community undermines faculty growth as well as student learning, especially when it comes to the evolution of pedagogy. There is a reason why the academy is still "delivering" most of its "product" in lecture form, a pedagogy that originated because books were rare and most people could not read. A professor who wants to evolve his or her way of teaching—which requires taking the risks that always accompany change—often has a hard time finding communal support for leaping into the unknown. Such people will continue to teach using the methods they know best, despite research that calls the effectiveness of those methods into question. When a teacher fears that taking a pedagogical risk and failing at it will lead to workplace marginalization or job insecurity, he or she must possess a rare degree of self-confidence to proceed.

But there is a way to support the evolution of professional practice, a tried-and-true model in, for example, high-tech companies. Here, people come together and ask, "What are we trying to do? How well are we doing it? What do we know about ways we might do it better? What kinds of risks do we need to take to find a better way forward?"

Once they reach consensus on these questions, they ask, "Who is willing to conduct an experiment designed around hypotheses that we all agree are worth testing, while we collect process and outcome data that will come back to the group for collective consideration? Who is willing to take some communally approved risks that might help all of us do our work better—not dumb risks but thoughtful risks based on a communal agreement about what is worth trying? These efforts may result in failures, but they will be failures from which all of us can learn."

That scenario portrays a climate in which thoughtful pedagogical evolution would thrive because experimenters are supported rather than isolated, and rewarded rather than punished for risk taking, even when they fail. But it is the rare college or university that offers its faculty such a climate. This is why the work of the Carnegie Foundation on "the scholarship of teaching and learning" is so important, not merely for its substantive findings but for its tested and proven disciplines for creating the communities of practice needed to evolve new pedagogies.[6]

The power of peer communities to help educational institutions grow their mission capacity is the focus of an important study of K-12 public education that deserves to be more widely known in higher

When Philosophy Is Put into Practice

education.[7] Sponsored by the Russell Sage Foundation, Anthony Bryk and Barbara Schneider looked at school reform efforts in Chicago across the decade of the 1990s. They asked a simple question: what factors led some Chicago schools to get better at teaching basic skills over that ten-year period while others either stayed flat or went south? They looked at all the usual suspects—curriculum, in-service training, budgets, models of governance, demographic factors—and found that none of them could explain the variations in success.

But they found one variable that had great explanatory power: they called it "relational trust," which I read as a synonym for "community." If a school had high relational trust and/or a leadership core that worked on trust-building, that school had roughly a five-out-of-seven chance of serving students better by the end of the decade. But if a school had low relational trust and/or a leadership cadre that ignored it, the chance of serving students better by the end of the decade sank to roughly two out of seven. This is a large statistical difference, and although it narrowed, it did not disappear when other variables were factored in. That is, you can toss a lot of money or state-of-the-art curricular materials into a school full of mutually distrustful people and you will not get appreciable improvement in mission performance.

Trust in Schools is an important study, one that should be widely read by all who care about strengthening the educational mission. At the same time, we need to ask, "Who doesn't know that a building full of people who don't trust each other will fail to help each other improve their professional practice no matter how many material resources you provide them?"

This is another one of those secrets hidden in plain sight that higher education needs to embrace, understand, and act upon if we want to advance our pedagogical practice and outcomes. It is an expression of the concept of community that is both the philosophical driver and the practical outcome of an integrative approach to education.

THE HEART OF HIGHER EDUCATION

CRITIQUE 5: ACADEMICS AND SPIRITUALITY DON'T MIX

The final critique I want to explore is that integrative education—which sometimes takes us beyond logic and data into the nonrational realms of religion and spirituality—threatens certain core values of intellectual life. Rationality and empiricism, say the critics, should never cohabit with religion or spirituality lest we lose the long-term historical gains of science over superstition, of objectivity over subjectivity.

Once again, the critics have an important point: remember Galileo. There are genuine dangers involved in mixing the religious and "secular" worlds, especially given the power of various fundamentalisms these days. As a Quaker whose spiritual ancestors were disproportionately represented in England's intellectual establishment *and* who came to this country only to be hanged on Boston Common by folks who were not altogether clear about the separation of church and state, I have no romance about the "good old days."

But precisely because these dangers exist, they demand public scrutiny, so religion and spirituality must be understood as critical parts of the human "mess" that higher education should help students engage. Excluding religion and spirituality from serious study in secular settings is a stunning form of irrationality in itself. Religion and spirituality are among the major drivers of contemporary life (as one can readily see in any daily newspaper) and of any historical epoch one can name.

Not long ago, a Harvard faculty task force proposed a new course called Rationality and Faith for the core curriculum.[8] The proposal failed because a majority of faculty argued that faith had no place as a subject of study in the academic curriculum. Louis Menand, professor of English and co-chair of the task force, summarized his group's response in words that are, I believe, the most cogent and concise ever uttered on this matter: "It's noncontroversial that there is this thing called religion out there and that it has an enormous

47

impact on the world we live in. Scholars should be able to study and teach it without getting cooties."[9]

My dictionary offers primary and secondary definitions of *religion* that tend to cohere in common usage: "(a) Belief in and reverence for a supernatural power or powers regarded as creator and governor of the universe. (b) A personal or institutionalized system grounded in such belief and worship." Clearly, personal and institutionalized religion has played a role in human history that is at least as prominent as princes, parliaments, and military power.

There is less consensus around the definition of *spirituality*, so I offer a well-tested definition of my own, a neutral definition in that it does not imply that spirituality is always something good or always something bad: "Spirituality is the eternal human yearning to be connected with something larger than one's own ego."

This "yearning" can connect us with great evil, as well as great good. The Third Reich was a form of spirituality in which people who felt their security slipping away from them were drawn toward the demonic god of "blood, soil, and race." The black liberation movement in this country was one in which spirituality took a quite different form, connecting us across lines of division rather than deepening those divisions in more and more murderous ways. Clearly, higher education ought to be inviting students to give thoughtful consideration to energy fields of both sorts on their way to a diploma.

At a deeper level of intellectual life, more than a few scholars have noticed that the great spiritual traditions, such as Buddhism, were centuries ahead of science in positing the interconnectedness of reality that physicists and others now proclaim. When academics are ignorant of this evolution of ideas from spiritual to scientific sources, the wellspring of that ignorance is, I believe, identical to the wellspring of religious ignorance: an orthodox belief system that refuses to engage certain kinds of data and interpretations. Both kinds of orthodoxy must be exposed to the light of day and given a chance to grow beyond themselves; an integrative higher education can play a role in that process of illumination.

Higher education's resistance to exploring the diverse ways in which people navigate their inner lives is baffling given its philosophical root system. Part of that root system traces back to Socrates, who said, famously, "The unexamined life is not worth living," providing all the rationale needed for academic inquiries into and reflection upon all things spiritual and religious. I would raise the stakes around this issue by tagging a small corollary onto this Socratic axiom: "If you choose to live an unexamined life, please do not take a job that involves other people!"

Higher education looses upon the world too many people who are masters of external, objective reality, with the knowledge and skill to manipulate it, but who understand little or nothing about inner drivers of their own behavior. Giving students knowledge as power over the world while failing to help them gain the kind of self-knowledge that gives them power over themselves is a recipe for danger—and we are living today with the proof of that claim in every realm of life from economics to religion. We need to stop releasing our students into the wild without systematically challenging them to take an inner as well as outer journey. Integrative education can help us do just that.

The Way We Die

I want to end my reflections on these large issues in the philosophy of education by bringing us back home to ourselves and to the way we die—a topic that provides a plumb line by which everything we do in education can and should be measured, or so it seems to me.

During one period of my life, I became fascinated with the Rule of Benedict, a classic fourth-century volume of guidance for the early monks as they began gathering in the desert to lay the foundations for the monasteries that can be found around the planet to this day. Among other things, these monasteries preserved critical artifacts of civilization, including books, during rabidly destructive periods of human history, forming yet another part of higher education's root system.

When Philosophy Is Put into Practice

There is much in the Rule of Benedict that I admire, not least Benedict's realism. For example, he urges the monks to receive all visitors with hospitality, including long-term guests, but he understands the possibility that a guest may disrupt monastic order. On the first such occasion, Benedict says, the Guest Master should counsel with the visitor and bid him be at peace. On the second occasion, the Abbot should speak to him more sternly, informing the guest that he must cease and desist if he wishes to stay on. On the third occasion, says Benedict, "two stout monks" should escort the guest to the gates and bid him never return. As I think about the importance of hospitality in the classroom, Benedict's counsel seems sound to me.

In that same spirit of realism, one of Benedict's rules says, "Daily keep your death before your eyes." When I first read that line at age thirty-five, it struck me as miserably morbid. But as I grew older, I began to realize that it is not morbid at all: rightly understood and practiced, it is a life-giving piece of advice. Cultivating a steady awareness of the fact that we will die can help us savor the gift of life and use it to the fullest.

In that spirit, I want to close this chapter with a quote from a great educator: the late James O. Freedman, president of Dartmouth College, who died of cancer in 2006. In 1994, at the outset of his journey with terminal illness, at a time when he knew that his death would come sooner and would likely be more painful than he had imagined, Freedman gave a commencement talk about his new-found understanding of liberal education "under the aspect of eternity." He might as well have been speaking about integrative education; what he had to say illumines and adds gravitas to everything I have been reaching for in this chapter. Here is the wisdom Freedman left for us to ponder en route to his own conscious death:

> Hearing a physician say the dread word *cancer* has an uncanny
> capacity to concentrate the mind. That is what liberal education
> does, too. God willing, both this disease and my liberal
> education will each, in its own way, prove to me a blessing.

THE HEART OF HIGHER EDUCATION

I have been struck by two realizations—first, that life is a learning process for which there is no wholly adequate preparation; second, that although liberal education is not perfect, it is the best preparation there is for life and its exigencies. It does indeed enable us better to make sense of the events that either break over us, like a wave, or quietly envelop us before we know it, like a drifting fog.

What, then, is the use of a liberal education? When the ground seems to shake and shift beneath us, liberal education provides perspective, enabling us to see life steadily and to see it whole.

It has taken an illness to remind me, in my middle age, of that lesson. But that is just another way of saying that life, like liberal education, continues to speak to us—if we have the stillness and the courage to listen. That reminder is worth more than gold.[10]

Chapter 3

Beyond the Divided Academic Life

Arthur Zajonc

My first encounter with what Parker Palmer calls "the divided life" took place when I was a college student. Upon arrival, the relentless activity of high school academics, sports, and family gave way to an independent and irregular life at the University of Michigan in Ann Arbor. At first the patterns of the earlier period held and I did well among the 35,000 students. I was excited equally by the promise of my mathematics, physics, chemistry, and Great Books courses; they would surely bring me closer to my unarticulated hope for a life of significance and purpose. But already by my second year I was floundering, and by my third year I was silently despondent. What was all this about? What did thermodynamics or German have to offer to quell the unsettling disorientation and longing I felt? The inchoate longing I felt went unaddressed; the meaning

I sought for in education, and in science particularly, remained unmet. I looked around desperately, but saw no place to land my lonely soul.

Around me, but at a distance, swirled the Vietnam War and the civil rights movement. Yet none of my outer activities, whether social or academic, possessed inner meaning. Inside of me was despair. Such was my state of mind at twenty. I was experiencing what Kronman and Lewis would write about decades later as the soullessness of the university that no longer views one of its tasks as offering "their students an education in the meaning of life."[1]

I could not reconcile myself to living a divided life that abandoned the hope of any vocation with real meaning. Rather than live a lie, I decided I should end my studies, with the likely consequence that I would be drafted and sent to Vietnam. I resolved to flunk out. I stopped turning in homework and left tests early. After my final examinations that semester, on a whim, I stopped by my physics professor's office. He was an older man, originally from Holland and with a formal manner, but in our class on Lagrangian dynamics a few remarks he had made some weeks earlier intrigued me. The conversation we had that day changed everything. It had two parts. The first concerned my poor performance in his class, which he recognized as a reflection of my deeper malaise. He understood my situation immediately, and his advice was pragmatic and clear. The second aspect of the conversation, however, was highly unusual and much more decisive. It concerned his own attempt at integrating meaning and purpose into his life as a scientist. We spoke soberly and seriously about matters ethical, spiritual, and scientific, all in a single conversation.

Here before me was a person who had worked for forty years to knit together in his own fashion an undivided life philosophy that embraced an experiential, contemplative spirituality. Not much of it showed in his classes, but enough that I unconsciously sought him out in my own time of trial.

What he shared with me that day, and in the months and years that followed, helped me to chart my own course toward an integrated life. Without him as a role model, and others I discovered through him, the subjects I was studying would have remained barren and senseless. (It was at this conversation with Professor Ernst Katz that I was introduced to the contemplative, spiritual philosopher Rudolf Steiner.) I could not have continued. But with the beginnings of an integrated life in hand, I found the old subjects filled with hidden significance and unexpected connections. The human dimensions of science, its spiritual implications and ethical aspects, began to dawn on me. I was drawn back into the drama and beauty of mathematics and physics, literature and philosophy. The content presented was unchanged, but the lens through which I read the texts, equations, and arguments revealed heretofore unnoticed significance and granted meaning to otherwise inert material. I learned to animate what I was receiving, and as Emerson once wrote, "We animate what we can, we see only what we animate. Nature and books belong to the eyes that see them."[2] My reanimated mode of engagement propelled me through graduate school, postdoctoral research, and animates me still as a physics teacher, researcher, and writer.

I simply could not live the divided life. Psychologically, I had fallen apart, or perhaps I had broken open. Had I not found a mentor, I would have left the university. Others of my peers adapted; they seemed to find a way to dull the sensation of loss and reconcile themselves to what life had brought. Those who refused to compromise traveled to India, or marched on Washington and Selma, or they overdosed.

The divided life of students was not a temporary phenomenon characteristic of the 1960s and 1970s; it is a perennial crisis common to all generations. As a college teacher for thirty years I have seen the cynicism in many of our bright first-year students who already have partly given up their youthful ideals and are settling for the goal of a six-figure starting salary. Under the surface they still hope, but gradually they lose the vision of a life in which work and ideals are united, where purpose and values are part of the way they earn their daily bread. Perhaps part of the allure of Barack and Michelle Obama is the story of a couple who did not give up, who found a way to live undivided: to practice law and serve their communities at the same time. They joined their ideals to their craft.

It is clear that the primary divide we are concerned with in this book is not the fragmentation of knowledge or the loss of community, as serious as these issues are (and we will treat them as well). These are symptoms of a deeper underlying divide within us, one that distribution requirements or learning communities alone, for example, will not address. Our colleges and universities need to encourage, foster, and assist our students, faculty, and administrators in finding their own authentic way to an undivided life where meaning and purpose are tightly interwoven with intellect and action, where compassion and care are infused with insight and knowledge. In some contexts it may make sense to distinguish between facts and values, but they should never be reified into divisions that fragment us and our world. Then the map we live by is a lie and a burden.

ATTENDING TO PURPOSE

While studying in Ann Arbor, I found that some of my most important learnings occurred through the relationships I made outside the classroom. But I was one of the fortunate ones. Integration and wholeness in student life is too important to be left to chance. It should be one of the guiding motives of higher education. Too frequently such integration is left to chance meetings like mine, or to those few teachers who take the system into their own hands and teach in ways that allow the idealism of youth to join with vocational mastery. Integration should be intentional and systemic, not accidental and extracurricular. The first step in rectifying this situation is through sustained conversations concerning the purposes of education at our colleges and universities (about which we will have more to say later). We speak together far too seldom about our aims for the education of our students. And when we do talk about pedagogy, it is too often on the most basic level of skills and content distribution requirements.

In his candid evaluation of *Our Underachieving Colleges*, one-time Harvard president Derek Bok calls this tendency "neglecting purposes."[3] As he aptly notes, our revision of the curriculum "begins without the parties having paid close enough attention to the objectives that a proper undergraduate education should pursue.... By not paying careful attention to purposes, faculties have also ignored important aims of undergraduate education over extended periods of time."[4] The aims of a college education are many, and so should be the conversations. One conversation worth having concerns the cultivation of imagination.

In his *Aims of Education* of 1929, Alfred North Whitehead declared that the university's task was the welding together of imagination and experience.[5] He saw imagination as a special gift of youth and experience as an attribute of a mature professoriate. He maintained that "the proper function of a university is the imaginative acquisition of knowledge.... A university is imaginative or it is nothing—at least nothing useful." While Whitehead, like many philosophers before him, appreciated the power of formal reasoning and the empirical foundations of science, he also recognized that nothing new can arise from deduction and induction alone. Once one possesses a theory, deductions can be drawn and checked against experiments, but no theory has ever been discovered by deduction. Likewise, as useful as data collection might be, it needs to serve a higher purpose. Data becomes ordered and meaningful only through imaginative insight. Einstein thought that the discovery of nature's laws requires the capacity of intuition and a heartfelt enthusiasm for the work:

> There is no logical path to these laws; only intuition, resting on
> sympathetic understanding of experience, can reach them....
> The state of mind which enables a man to do work of this kind
> is akin to that of the religious worshiper or the lover; the daily
> effort comes from no deliberate intention or program, but
> straight from the heart.[6]

Elsewhere he famously maintained that "imagination is more important than knowledge. For knowledge is limited, whereas imagination embraces the entire world, stimulating progress, giving birth to evolution."[7] Or in the words of Einstein's contemporary

Beyond the Divided Academic Life

and scientific peer Henri Poincaré, "It is by logic we prove, it is by intuition we invent."[8] Appreciating the role of imagination in making discoveries, Whitehead insisted that it should be at the heart of higher education. Yet Whitehead also warned that the life of imaginative scholarship, research, and education is always under the threat of "inert ideas" or dead knowledge:

> We must be aware of what I will call "inert ideas"—that is to say, ideas that are merely received into the mind without being utilized, or tested, or thrown into fresh combinations . . . . Education with inert ideas is not only useless; it is, above all things, harmful . . . . Every intellectual revolution which has ever stirred humanity into greatness has been a passionate protest against inert ideas. Then, alas, with pathetic ignorance of human psychology, it has proceeded by some educational scheme to bind humanity afresh with inert ideas of its own fashioning.[9]

As Whitehead points out, a pedagogy anchored too strongly in tradition is bound to inert ideas. While the ideas and artistic productions of the past are invaluable, to keep them relevant and open to our imagination, we must test them, make them new, and contribute our own original thoughts and productions to posterity. A challenge for integration in education is this joining of past experience with the innovative spirit of the present. Universities should be a prime venue for such imaginative and integrative work, where a true stimulus in the direction of new insights and creations is given to the minds and hearts of those who are part of its community.

What would a pedagogy look like that supports and encourages imagination? This question could be a rich topic for a conversation concerning the purpose of an undergraduate education that reaches beyond vocation and citizenship to the cultivation of one's full humanity. From the side of literature and art, we might be reminded of Keats's important notion of "negative capability," which can sustain ambiguity and even contradiction "without any irritable reaching after fact and reason."[10] From the side of science, we might hear voices in support of fact and reason, but acknowledge with Einstein and Poincaré the value of imagination. Conversations of this type are not run by Robert's Rules of Order, nor is closure expected—to truly engage in this kind of cross-discipline inquiry, we must be willing to engage in the more expansive and exploratory conversation with our colleagues that is at the heart of this book. For without these conversations, and the questions and explorations they prompt, an institution's values remain obscure and a faculty rudderless.

THE ARGUMENT: A SKETCH

Since the sixteenth century the twin forces of science and the Industrial Revolution have played an important role in shaping the picture we have of the world and each other. Education since then has taken place within that emerging scientific and technical worldview, with profound consequences. Science and the development of a vibrant industrial economy have brought enormous advances in education to many millions around the world who have become literate and numerate for the first time in history. And yet, the myopic vision of science and industry has also failed our students and our future. The ways in which we educate students today are, in large part, a reflection of our worldview, which itself is an image of nineteenth-century science. In this view, knowledge is largely inert and objective, and education is limited to teaching students how to manipulate the knowledge they accumulate at school. The arts have long suffered under this distortion of learning. Additionally, the social embeddedness and ethical implications of our knowledge are largely overlooked. This distortion arises in part due to a mistaken and outdated conception of science, so I will be at pains in this book to indicate exactly how the new sciences support the need for an expanded ontology and enriched epistemology. The richly interconnected world's depictions by the new physics and ecology are but two examples of the fresh worldview now required. The future transformation of education against the background of this new imagination may well be as profound as any we have known since the rise of the modern university.

In the following pages the argument I wish to make is simply this: our current educational philosophy is based on a dominant and largely unconscious worldview that is both outmoded and limiting. In particular we teach our students to distrust direct experience in favor of hidden insular entities and discrete causal factors that cognition can represent but never directly reveal. In this view, students are denied direct experiential access to the truth of their world and must contend with models of reality instead. There is nothing harmful in this as long as we—faculty and students alike—do not mistake our models for reality (Whitehead's "misplaced concreteness"), but too often this caution is neglected. In the current configuration, truth, the goal of education, is seen to be attained only when we have reduced appearance to these entities and factors, and the mechanistic relationships between them. I argue that the new physics opposes this misguided view, and I show how modern science asserts the primacy of experience and relationships that are not reducible to entities and mechanisms. And I show how, if experience is indeed core to human reality, then the task of education is the refinement and extension of experience into both the outer and inner dimensions of human life. Insight too is appreciated in this view as an epiphanic experience and not an exercise in logic. Once one entertains such a view, the implications for higher education are significant, and I detail some of these in subsequent chapters.

The framework I present is consistent with the view voiced by Parker Palmer in response to the critics of integrative education. It has become for me a guiding framework for an integrative approach to higher education, one that recognizes the whole human being and his or her place in community and the world. By seeing the cultivation of human experience as the basis of education, we multiply our ways of knowing ("epistemology"), and enrich our understanding of the world ("ontology"). Truth and compassion are recognized as irreducible human experiences that become the basis for genuine ethical action.

THE HEART OF HIGHER EDUCATION

I also wrestle with the thorny question of the right relationship between spirituality and the education of adults, which is unavoidable once we concern ourselves with meaning, purpose, and the whole human. As Palmer rightly recognizes, we need to step back to consider these larger perspectives if we are to achieve the coherence we seek for integrative education. The rush to technique, to problem-solve pressing educational dilemmas, can obscure the indispensable need for a truly adequate foundation if our pedagogies are to serve the real aims of higher education. In subsequent chapters and appendices, with the help of several contributors, we feature particular efforts that have been made toward realizing a more integrative undergraduate education. But in the remainder of this chapter I take up the philosophical infrastructure sketched by Parker Palmer in the first two chapters and develop it in more detail. Against this background, the many diverse pedagogical interventions can begin to cohere to one another, forming a comprehensive integrative education, so that what has been seen as an assortment of valuable but discrete techniques can be understood as the expression of an implicit underlying educational philosophy.

EXPANDING OUR UNIVERSE

If we would expand the worldview that supports education, we can find no better place to begin than by opening ourselves to the full scope of human experience. Life comprises an infinitely rich array of sensorial, emotional, and intellectual experiences. Whether walking beside a forest stream or listening to the premiere of a new opera, whether contra dancing or working at a laboratory bench, the theater of the mind is dense with impressions, feelings, thoughts, and impulses toward action. Parallel to the universe of outer experience is a comparably rich world of inner experience. Taken together they constitute the world of *human experience*. Strangely though, reductive philosophy and science, even higher education, seem bent on gutting the richness of experience, reducing it to evolutionary

Beyond the Divided Academic Life

adaptive strategies and synapse firings. Experience has been labeled "epiphenomenal" and considered by some to be merely the froth on the wave of a neuro-physical reality. Yet it is here that we live our lives, that we suffer and rejoice, struggle to understand, to love, to act.

Twenty years ago I was at a reception for distinguished Amherst College alumni. While there I fell into conversation with the head of Harvard's biology department. He heard that I was in physics and said to me, "Yours is the only real science, and I have done everything I could to force out those in my department who practiced traditional biology of whole organisms in favor of molecular biologists. That is real science, the rest is garbage." His attitude and actions reflected the dominance of molecular and atomic thinking that had displaced the study of organisms and ecosystems. Only recent environmental catastrophes have led to a modest resurgence of research and teaching concerning the environment and whole organisms at our university science departments.

Ironically, as our exploration of the universe has progressed and our understanding of its contents and history has improved, our perception and the value of it have become diminished. We can see back in time 12 billion years with our telescopes and detect the faint afterglow of the Big Bang with our sensitive rocket-borne instruments; we can identify black holes, quasars, exoplanets, dark matter, and dark energy. Atoms and subatomic particles give up their secrets under scanning tunneling microscopes and in our giant colliders. Yet for all the variety, we see these objects as of a single type. At least in the popular imagination, they are all viewed as matter in combinations, large and small. The many layers of the "great chain of being," whose history was notably recounted by Arthur O. Lovejoy, once spanned the universe from minerals and plants to humans and beyond, but now it has collapsed to a single all-encompassing, commonplace element.[11] Where many cultures over many centuries saw a hierarchy of being, we now see the sole remnant as an inert substance which, when compounded and set in motion, is thought to give rise to the epiphenomena of life and mind, values and purpose. Gone are life, consciousness, soul, and spirit. This view reflects itself in innumerable ways in the priorities and methods sanctioned throughout the academy.

The humanities are not immune to this mindset; it merely goes under another name. Robert Bellah and colleagues cite a graduate-student orator who, in his commencement address, lamented: "They tell us that it is heresy to suggest the superiority of some value, fantasy to believe in moral arguments, slavery to submit to a judgment sounder than your own. The freedom of our day is the freedom to devote ourselves to any values we please on the mere condition that we do not believe them to be true."[12]

Too often, in the wake of postmodern deconstruction, a radical pluralistic confusion and an oddly playful nihilism are all that remains. The important insights concerning the social construction and content of texts are swamped by an iconoclastic zeal that slays meaning wherever it arises. Since the 1980s, I have sat across from some of Amherst College's brightest students who, having mastered the philosophy and techniques of deconstruction advocated by Derrida, Foucault, and Lacan, lamented the subsequent loss of meaning and sought ways to regain the value of the texts themselves and a purpose to their lives. One summa student rejected attractive graduate school offers in order to take up public service law, where he felt he might do some real good and leave the emptiness of literature, as he had been taught it, behind. While we may reject Allan Bloom's utopian version of higher education's glorious past, his critique of its current soullessness strikes home for many.

What counts as serious academic research, good teaching, and success have too long been reduced to a truncated or fragmented understanding of the world. This would be fine if we knew it to be true, but in fact we now know that the universe is far richer, more subtle, and more interconnected than reductionism allows. Conventional materialist notions and the radical deconstruction of texts, persons, and communities no longer hold, and a new view is emerging that reinstates Lovejoy's chain of being in a new guise and grants a renewed standing to experience. We are now called to develop a view of higher education that simultaneously values the self-consciousness of the new science, literary criticism, philosophy,

Beyond the Divided Academic Life

sociology, and anthropology without extremism while also affirming the possibility of a way to truth, meaning, and purpose. Not all values should be sanctioned, not all moral arguments are equal, and the cultivation of our humanity leads not only to painful self-knowledge but also to greater wisdom and compassion. The consequences of an expanded ontology for the university will be profound if we take it to heart.

DANGERS OF A TRUNCATED WORLDVIEW

Before detailing a few of the arguments for and the features of this expansive ontology, it is important to reflect on the potential harm of a truncated view of ourselves and our world, and the benefits of an integrated one.

Each day for one week in 1997, five other scientists and I explored the intersection of Buddhist philosophy with cosmology and the new physics.[13] The setting was the private quarters of the Dalai Lama in Dharamsala, India. In attendance were twenty Tibetan monk-scholars from various monastic universities and the Dalai Lama. For years the Dalai Lama has been deeply committed to expanding the scope of his understanding to include the full range of new scientific phenomena and theories. He explained to us that ignorance is the root cause of suffering and that genuine open-minded inquiry into the nature of reality can be of great benefit to humanity by dispelling that ignorance. For this reason he was eager to expand his already prodigious philosophical and meditative knowledge to include modern science. And he especially hoped we would find ways to help educate his young monk-scholars in the new sciences as well. He held that *all* aspects of the world, outer and inner, coarse and subtle, body and mind, are open to human investigation, and a full understanding of them is required for the mitigation of suffering. Partial understanding implies ignorance of some aspects of reality and so inevitably leads to continued suffering. Only comprehensive insight into the true nature of the human being and the world can provide the basis for release from the delusions that lead to suffering, he explained. For these reasons he hoped that

THE HEART OF HIGHER EDUCATION

the curriculum at Buddhist monastic universities could be changed to include science. Our collaboration with the Dalai Lama and his monk-scholars has continued for over twenty-five years through the work of the Mind and Life Institute.

My dialogues with the Dalai Lama and others live in me as vibrant examples of what an authentic faculty conversation might look like. The motivation is clear from the outset. Instead of curiosity or financial gain, the aim is for a knowing that will reduce suffering. To this end all aspects of human experience are granted equal consideration. The intellectual standards are very high, but no view is ruled out on the basis of metaphysical precommitments. As a consequence the full richness of the world, inner as well as outer, spiritual as well as material, is able to be freely explored. One feels that through such openness, combined with sober reasoning and attention to experience, everything is possible. I have felt far greater freedom in these meetings than in my thirty years in the academy, where fear is a frequent specter that encumbers free speech.

If precommitments or fears dominate our thinking, we deny ourselves valuable avenues of inquiry, and dismiss, for example, the thousands of years of contemplative exploration contained in the Asian traditions. Our view of the mind and the world is partial as a consequence of seeing it only from our limited Western viewpoint. If we possess only a partial truth, then when we approach problems in the environment, medicine, education, economics, mental health, and so on, we do so from a limited viewpoint. Our current conception of higher education and the treatment of our students derive from just such a fragmentary and incomplete understanding. We do not have the whole student in mind before us; too often students are seen only in part. As a consequence, our well-intended programs and pedagogy are predicated on a partial and thus inadequate view. A diminished ontology is a powerful distorting lens that obscures the true multidimensional reality of our world, hiding the full scope of our humanity and the deeper complexity of our world. Genuine solutions, adequate to our problems—personal, societal, and environmental—will only arise from an expanded ontology that embraces the richness that is the universe.

SCIENTIFIC SUPPORT
FOR AN EXPANDED ONTOLOGY

As Parker Palmer points out in Chapter 1, in recent years the reasons for broadening our ontology have become increasingly scientific. We have long had philosophical objections to materialist reductionism, but now physics has added its voice and redirects our attention to experience. I would like to amplify Palmer's remarks concerning what physics can offer to our considerations.

Through certain carefully designed experiments and theoretical analysis, physics can undertake what the philosopher and physicist Abner Shimony has called an "experimental metaphysics." The issues which philosophers have debated for centuries are, in some instances, now open to experimental investigation, and the results of that research are profound. From sensitive experiments in quantum mechanics and relativity, we are forced to abandon a naïve materialistic paradigm in favor of one that puts experience in the place of objects, and sees relationships no longer as mediated solely by conventional forces between isolated entities; a deeper holism is at play. The architects of the "new physics"—Heisenberg, Einstein, Bohr, and Schrödinger, among others—struggled mightily with the implications of their discoveries at the dawn of the twentieth century, but only recently has experimental and technical prowess advanced to the point where the full implications of quantum theory and relativity can be explored and even harnessed for technological applications. As a result, the speculations of the founders have been clarified and the full implications of the new physics realized. These implications extend all the way to the philosophical heart of higher education.

We begin with the fallacy of the disconnected onlooker, which is underscored by Einstein's theory of special relativity. Science since Locke and Newton had privileged spatial extension and mass over "secondary qualities" like color and sound. But relativity theory and its supporting experiments demonstrate that even primary qualities like extension, mass, and temporal duration depend fundamentally on the relative states of motion between observer and observed.

Relativity of simultaneity, length contraction, and time dilation show that lengths are shortened along their direction of motion, and moving clocks run slow. Lengths and temporal intervals thus depend on the frame of reference in which they are measured. Since no frame of reference is privileged in relativity theory, we must give up our notion of objects possessing inherent objective attributes like size, shape, mass, and rate of change. We need to learn to see these as existing through a *relationship* with the observer, not as attributes of the "thing-in-itself." Indeed, I would go so far as to say that all of the attributes by which we identify objects only arise through relationship to an observer, real or imagined.

There is no privileged, God's-eye view that can see the true state of affairs. In fact, no relationship-free "true" state of affairs exists. Yet we do have a godlike power, and that is the power to change our vantage point. We can circle the subject of interest, gaining with each new perspective another view in. If we do this with care, each experience exposes another side of the reality we seek. Instead of thinking of the universe as composed of minute hidden particles modeled on sense objects, we begin to experience the potent creative agency in the universe that can manifest in such varied phenomena once a relationship is established. We shift from viewing nature as object to nature as activity, from *natura naturata* (nature natured) to *natura naturans* (nature naturing), as Spinoza called it.

The new physics encourages an epistemology that knits together the observer and the creative world in an indissoluble manner. In his book on special relativity, David Bohm summarizes the implications of Einstein's theory by saying "the analysis of the world into constituent objects has been replaced by its analysis in terms of events and processes."[14] Objects conceived of as nonphenomenal material bodies are unsupportable; phenomena are all we have. This gives a whole new significance to the so-called epiphenomena of consciousness. In our search for more fundamental components to nature, we can never "get behind" phenomena. Atoms are no different, in this regard, from the pebbles on the beach. They are real because they have attributes. They are like

the "objects" of everyday life, which certainly exist, but as phenomenal entities in relationship to a group of observers. The phenomena
we experience are simultaneously a reflection of world reality and
of our specific state of mind. Thus, education should be, in part, the
cultivation of the mind so that the breadth and depth of the world
can be explored.

QUANTUM HOLISM

Quantum physics underscores this essential connection between the
observer and the observed. Heisenberg points to this when he states,
"The object of research is no longer nature itself but man's investigation of nature."[15] Quantum physicist Niels Bohr emphasizes
"the essential wholeness of a proper quantum phenomenon," and
he declares that in quantum physics the interaction between object
and the measuring instrument "forms an inseparable part of the
phenomenon."[16] The act of observation is, therefore, an essential and
constitutive dimension of the phenomenon. The observer is impli-
cated in every phenomenon, and we need to resist the temptation
to seek an object that is nonphenomenal and observer-independent
behind the phenomena. Experience, to paraphrase William James,
is what we have first, foremost, and always. It can be varied and
cultivated through the intention and practice of the person, but
experience is James's and science's bedrock.

Once we take this view seriously (and it is the one increasingly
supported by a thoughtful examination of our fundamental sciences),
we realize that there is no getting around the experiential or
phenomenological nature of all knowledge. The forest stream, the
opera, and the atom all have standing by virtue of their experiential
aspect, which arises in relationship to us. *The implications of this view
of reality for education are great.* It can pivot the entire mandate of
university inquiry away from a privileged objectivist and material
metaphysics to an egalitarian one of connection, relationship, and
lived experience. The full scope of our humanity, which we seek to
cultivate, is included in this orientation toward the world. Through
our teaching, we can attempt to extend experience, make it more

reliable, and seek after the hidden interrelationships in experience through reason and reflection. This is the real work of science as well as the other disciplines.

The contemporary physicist Anton Zeilinger, winner of the Newton Prize, has put forward an ontology of information or knowledge that supports this view:

> [O]ne may be tempted to assume that whenever we ask questions of nature, of the world there outside, there is reality existing independently of what can be said about it. We will now claim that such a position is void of any meaning. It is obvious that any property or feature of reality out there can only be based on information we receive. There cannot be any statement whatsoever about the world or about reality that is not based on such information. It therefore follows that the concept of a reality without at least the ability in principle to make statements about it to obtain information about its features is devoid of any possibility of confirmation or proof. This implies that the distinction between information, that is, knowledge, and reality is devoid of any meaning.[17]

Contrary to conventional expectations, science is actually not about a pre-given, hidden, microscopic world existing completely independent of us, but it is about what we can know through experience and reason. The conscious human being is inextricably entangled with reality, when reality is taken as indistinguishable from information or knowledge. Here we see how physicists are increasingly shifting away from an ontology of matter and force to one of information or knowledge, where knowledge itself is not an object, but is an event. Thus education is at its heart not the conveyance of information concerning objects, but a leading of the inquiring minds of our students through the manifold layers of experience and reason to occasions of epiphany, that is, to the exalted experience of genuine insight. This is the joy of discovery that brightens students' faces and for which we teachers are rightly grateful. Experience may begin with the simplest observation, yet when elaborated and deepened through reflection, reason, and further observation, we do not leave the realm of experience but come to its highest expression in insightful understanding.

ATTENDING TO EXPERIENCE, CULTIVATING INSIGHT

The return to experience can seem like the abandonment of truth, but it is not. The cosmos is still an orderly home to countless species and lives, and not a universe of caprice and chaos. Einstein was a faithful thinker who followed reason wherever it led no matter how alien the territory. Within the unfolding multiplicity of viewpoints posited by the new physics is a hidden harmony between the knowledge of one observer and all others that weaves the universe together into a dynamic whole whose faces are many but whose core is single. The new physics is no mere language game, but it does urge us to recognize our place in the genesis of a life-world, which is our world of experience.

We are thus called back to the centrality of human experience in all its forms. The implications of this ontological shift for education are profound and call for a realignment of our priorities. The lost chain of being reemerges because each domain has equal standing, inasmuch as they are based equally on experience and reason. Whole organism biology and ecology have equal standing with molecular genetics if their observations are of comparable quality and scope. Likewise psychology has as much legitimacy as neuroscience; literature is as real as computational linguistics. The predominance of the hard science approach has been based on a metaphysical precommitment. Now we know that that commitment is flawed, and what matters is the care and range of the observations within a field of inquiry and the quality of thought that has been applied to the field. Thus there are excellent reasons, both philosophical and practical, for Harvard's biology department to give equal emphasis to whole organisms and ecology as to molecular biology. In fact, one can begin to detect this reversal already throughout the academy.

THE HEART OF HIGHER EDUCATION

If we move from an ontology of objects to one of insight, then a wide range of excluded or denigrated dimensions of human life moves into prominence. For example, inner human experiences such as trust and jealousy, love and hate, aspiration and depression all become legitimate areas of inquiry. They no longer need to be explained solely in terms of neuroscience or biochemistry, but rather they can come to have an ontological standing on par with the data of the hard sciences. What distinguishes the hard sciences from the softer sciences is not the subject of study (neurons versus emotions, for example) but the reliability of the data. When observations are variable and uncertain, then knowledge is likewise insecure. The challenge to the soft sciences, which depend on qualitative assessment, is to ensure that their observations are accurate and reproducible. In my view, all data is in some measure "subjective"; the challenge is to make the subjective something we can count on.

The mind is at the core of our human nature, our humanity. Yet its direct exploration by introspection has been off-limits for a century. This can change. In order to place inner experiences on equal footing with the knowledge of physics, we need not reduce the former to the latter. Rather, it is sufficient to make more secure and reliable our insights into our inner experience. Once these are rigorously studied by an aspect of our own mind, made into a stable and reliable instrument, and confirmed by others who have been comparably trained, then the facts of the inner life will have the same standing as the facts of the outer world.

The Dalai Lama was pointing to this when at a Mind and Life meeting with cognitive scientists he stated, "Not so long ago many people viewed science's objective knowledge and the subjective understanding of inner science as mutually exclusive. But a combination of these two can provide the complete conditions for obtaining real human happiness."[18] The "inner science" of which the Dalai Lama was speaking concerns the careful study of the mind by Buddhist monk-scholars over centuries using highly refined meditative methods for examining thought, emotion, consciousness, and the like. Contemplative methods, which can be entirely secular in character, represent an important form of inquiry that would

71

enhance a first-person, participatory epistemology, but they have largely been excluded from the academy. Alan Wallace, who has been educated both as a contemplative and a scholar, has termed science's rejection of the introspective method for the investigation of mental phenomena as "the taboo of subjectivity."[19] He has argued persuasively for the inclusion of the subjective in research and teaching, and this is supported by the thinking I have introduced above.

Neuroscientist Francisco Varela and philosopher Evan Thompson have long championed a combination of third-person and first-person methods for the study of the mind.[20] Each offers insights into the mind and together they can corroborate and illuminate each other. This points to the benefit of an enriched participatory epistemology and an education designed to stabilize the mind and strengthen our introspective powers of observation. William James viewed the cultivation of attention as education par excellence. In his classic treatise *The Principles of Psychology* he declared,

> [T]he faculty of voluntarily bringing back a wandering
> attention, over and over again, is the very root of judgment,
> character, and will . . . . An education which would improve this
> faculty would be *the* education par excellence. But it is easier to
> define this ideal than to give practical directions for bringing it
> about.[21]

Practical directions are increasingly available for the cultivation of attention. Inclusion of the contemplative training of attention has already begun to gain ground in higher education under the name of contemplative pedagogy and is a promising addition to our repertoire of pedagogical strategies.[22]

We have begun to expand our understanding of the world, its intrinsic worth, and our own value as human beings. The inner world of subjective experience is beginning to be considered as a domain of cultivation and research as valid as the outer. The consequences of this change of scope will be significant for expanding our view of ways of knowing, and it will also be of enormous help in navigating the difficult question of the relationship between science and spirituality in the academy.

Elizabeth Baron, a student at Brown University, sent us the following essay which points to the richness that is added when contemplative training is brought into the college classroom:

I can no longer imagine life without contemplative or meditative practice. I came to a large, research-oriented institution after 8 years at a small, Quaker private school that valued silence and communal contemplative practice. Entering a world in which others were not accustomed to reflective, silent experiences was jostling and unnerving. Education that focused on theory without encouraging practice always felt superficial and incomplete; it is necessary to strike a balance between learning from rich knowledge produced by others and from the wealth of insigh that exists within each individual.

At university, I struggled with my own educational experience, frustrated by the gap between intellectual work and experience. My third semester of college, I took a course on Buddhist Meditation with a meditation component, and found my life—academic, personal and social—transformed! Looking inwards and sitting with myself completely changed my eating, sleep and work habits for the better. Training in attention improved my work-ethic and study skills. Contemplative practice has helped me stay grounded and centered at a competitive, fast paced university.

Further, and perhaps most importantly, it woke me up to the importance of taking care of myself. I now genuinely believe that self-knowledge and self-reflection is invaluable to doing good work in this world. Awareness of my inner condition informs and inspires my external interactions—with growing knowledge of myself, I am better equipped to serve the world.

Through contemplative experiences within the classroom, my skepticism and cynicism towards formal education has been transformed to an aspiration for myself to become an educator of sorts. I was so profoundly affected by contemplative practice in the classroom that I designed my own major in contemplative education.

My passion to inspire social change is ignited by insight I gain into my own depth and consciousness. In a world with so many complex, interwoven problems, how can one come to an understanding and inspire sustainable, holistic change in the world without trying to do that to oneself?

MAKING IT REAL

I started this chapter with my story as an isolated student seeking meaning at the University of Michigan, and the importance of finding a mentor who helped me discover meaning both personally and in my studies. After the above philosophical considerations, I would like to reground the discussion by relating the experiences of two colleagues who have long labored to provide a more integrative, transformative, and humane environment for teaching and learning. The first is a story related by Sharon Daloz Parks, who has been a faculty member at the Schools of Divinity and Business and the Kennedy School of Government at Harvard University. She has written extensively on mentoring and the search for meaning by young adults.[23] In a piece written for us (see Appendix B), she recalls the potential power of learning when that learning is integrated into community life:

> This consciousness of the role of the social world in the formation of the intellect is a critical feature in the great adventure of teaching and learning. At this threshold time in history, if we are going to encourage the formation of the citizenship and leadership that is now required, we must pay close attention to the social contexts in which we learn and teach.

The second contribution I would like to point to addresses the challenge of anonymity, the distance between students and, in this case, the administration of a large public university. Jon Dalton has served as dean of students at Iowa State University and as vice president of student affairs at Florida State University. As Dalton points out, "One of the greatest challenges to integrating learning in large institutional settings in higher education is creating an environment that enables students to feel noticed and included." (See Appendix C for the full text of Dalton's contribution.) Through his actions Dalton demonstrated the concrete ways that faculty, students, and administration can break through the conventional structures of higher education to connect to one another directly and to develop the fuller dimensions of our humanity in community.

Chapter 4

Attending to Interconnection, Living the Lesson

Arthur Zajonc

How does one see a painting whole? Or the human mind? Or an ecosystem? Or for that matter, the educational project itself? We are well schooled in "seeing them" into parts—into brushstrokes, neurons, and molecules—or seeing the university apart into departments, disciplines, and specializations. What kind of attentiveness will enable us to see a true whole? What is the pedagogy for beholding interconnectedness as a primary reality and not a derived one? What are the implications of a deep experience of interconnection for knowing, teaching, learning, and life? What would be gained if, as the Dalai Lama says, we were to cultivate "a deep sense of caring for others, based on a profound sense of interconnection?"[1] It is perhaps difficult to appreciate how extensive the changes would be if this integrative viewpoint were fully embraced in higher education. The conventional view that privileges a single reductive perspective is so pervasive that undoing its effects will be difficult, but if we were to succeed, then the fragmentation of our education and our lives would be healed. Simultaneous with our experience of self would be the powerful complementary experience of human interdependence, of what Desmond Tutu calls *ubuntu*: "I exist because of you."

EMERGING WHOLES

Since Galileo, science has had a bias towards simplification for the very sensible and practical reason that it was all it could handle. Nothing is wrong with this as long as the limitation of the method is not projected onto reality, limiting it. If all you have is a thermometer, then everything is a temperature. But we now know that analysis of climate, the human nervous system, economics, and ant colonies, to mention only four examples, resist such simplification. To understand them with any subtlety requires that we embrace their inherent complexity and work with it. Until the last few decades, the exclusive method of studying complex systems was to break them down into fundamental parts and then to connect neighboring parts by means of simple forces. The forces between these distinct parts bind them into wholes. The whole is a mere amalgam of conjoined parts that has no ontological standing of its own. The solar system, in this view, comprises a star (the Sun), planets, asteroids, comets, and the like, all held together by the force of gravity acting between them. The atom likewise consists of a nucleus and surrounding electrons bound together by an electromagnetic force. This lens is then extended to chemistry, biology, and the human being. The parts are considered to be "real," as are the forces that make connections between the parts, but the whole—be it a mineral substance, plant, animal, or human—is a kind of chimera. While such a view is useful in many instances, we now know it to be fundamentally mistaken. Two scientific developments—entanglement and emergence (as well as common sense)—have made this conception of the world obsolete.

The first breakthrough came when physicists were able to attend to two things at once. This may sound simple, but to simultaneously measure the subtle properties of two or more quantum particles required a significant increase in resources and experimental sophistication. The simplest experiment of this type was first suggested in 1935 by Einstein, Rosen, and Podolsky,[2] but it had to wait until the 1980s for a definitive test. Light not only has the properties of intensity and color, but it can also have an internal orientation. If thought of as a wave, then the vibration can be up and down or side to side. These two different orientations of vibration are called *polarizations*. When physicists measured the correlations between the polarizations of photon pairs, the patterns in the data could not be explained by any classical conception of light. (The quantity measured is a complex correlation function for the probability of simultaneously detecting two photons at a particular polarization angle relative to one another.) The results were astounding, not because they required a new physical theory (quantum theory was adequate to the task), but because of their ontological implications. Here was a potent metaphysical experiment, and it demonstrated convincingly that the understanding we had of wholes as merely parts juxtaposed and bound together by forces was wrong. In a crucial manner, when two particles interact, they form an inseparable whole and the very attributes by which we would normally distinguish the one from the other become, as physicists term it, "entangled."[3] The two particles form a whole that is as real as the parts. Parts are no longer privileged.

I think it symbolic that wholes only showed themselves when physicists learned to attend to two things at once. The old practice of attending first to one thing (planet or particle) and then to another fragmented the world into parts. We were unconsciously practicing a particular kind of attention. The universe was and is a whole, but the method by which we chose to observe the universe fragmented it, and we mistakenly assumed our method gave us a true reflection of reality. In the process of learning how to attend to the whole, we learned that the experimental context and our kind of attention are highly significant: they cannot be excluded as inconsequential.

Attending to Interconnection, Living the Lesson

As we have seen already, our method of inquiry shapes, in part, the phenomena themselves, and it is only these phenomena to which we have access. If we attend to separate parts, that is what we see. If we are interested in wholes and devise an experimental method suited to that interest, then wholes show themselves. This is no mere relativism or pure constructivism, but rather an example of the world's richness that reveals itself in stages in response to us and our properly posed questions.

The best known physics example of the relationship between question and phenomenon is wave-particle duality. If the question we pose is "where is the photon?" then light shows itself as a particle. If, however, we do not ask "where?" but allow for an ambiguous trajectory for light, then the resulting observed interference pattern can best be understood in terms of light as a wave. These contradictory manifestations of light—first particle and then wave—arise in response to the experimental arrangement, which itself is the embodiment of a question. Classically considered, wave and particle are mutually exclusive concepts, but in quantum mechanics each aspect arises within a distinct measurement context and so it is entirely appropriate to that specific context. Context trumps consistency. The context in which we examine light fundamentally shapes the phenomenal manifestation, as well as our conception of light in that context.

The second scientific development that supports the overthrow of reductionism is emergence. If we turn in our imagination to walk along a lively forest stream, or if we listen to a Mozart aria we know well, it seems clear that our life is not made up of atoms and neurons but of a dense, rich array of meaningful experiences. What is the relation between the parts so often at the center of the scientists' attention, and the experience of wholes that occupy the rest of us? While the fact of quantum entanglement is a principled block to reductionism, a second scientific realization grants added weight to the status of wholes. Briefly put, scientists now recognize that the qualities that emerge in complex systems are often not able to be reduced to the parts that make up the system. Hydrogen and oxygen are the elemental gases that make up water, but the "wetness" of

THE HEART OF HIGHER EDUCATION

water is an "emergent property" of the system not reducible to hydrogen and oxygen.

In a seminal paper aptly titled "More Is Different," the Nobel physicist Philip Anderson stated, "At each level entirely new properties appear.... Psychology is not applied biology, nor is biology applied chemistry.... We can now see that the whole becomes not merely more, but very different from the sum of its parts."[4] Nobel physicist Robert Laughlin put it another way: "We live not at the end of discovery but at the end of Reductionism, a time in which the false ideology of human mastery of all things through microscopics is being swept away by events and reason."[5] Reductionism is, indeed, a false ideology. While we surely learn a great deal by attending to microscopic parts, we must be careful not to fall in love with the myopic view that mode of analysis offers. We must complement it with an equal attention to relationships and wholes. Only then will we truly behold the painting, appreciate the mind, and understand the complex reality that is the ecosystem. Only then can we arrive at a pedagogy that sees students as whole and complex beings and educates students with an eye to this reality.

In summary, I have used science to expand our worldview beyond a reductive materialist ontology in two ways.[6] First, Einstein's relativity and quantum mechanics both undermine objectification and support a *relational view of reality* in which phenomena are co-created by the observer and the world. Second, through entanglement and emergence, physics offers evidence for an *ontological holism* that grants wholes a standing long denied them. Parts are no longer privileged. These two realizations are essential to a proper philosophical infrastructure for higher education.

PEDAGOGIES OF EXPERIENCE AND INTERCONNECTION

Nearly every subject area in the academy has attempted to make itself over into a "science" by adopting its own version of the worldview and methods of the old physics of objectification and disconnection. Along the way, the education of the whole human being in community and the cultivation of his or her humanity seem to be increasingly forgotten for the sake of scientific simplification. If we take Laughlin and others seriously, then these fields need to reconceive themselves according to a postreductionist paradigm in which lived experience, connection, and complexity are given far more attention. Every field will also benefit from adopting ways of teaching and learning that are in closer alignment with the relational and integrative view of reality we now possess. In this regard, consider economics, health care, and medical education.

Economics has long objectified the human being, reduced to an idealized *homo economicus*, a hypothetical rational actor who maximizes his or her utility function (which mathematically represents the preferences of the consumer). In addition, our relationships to fellow members of our community are reduced to the limited concept of the market. With these two abstractions of the human being and communal relations, economics performs its analysis. While a useful formal model, classical economic theory of this kind has come in for heavy criticism and much modification. As in physics, the simplifying assumptions of classical economics were made because economic theory could not handle the complexities of the real world. But are humans really rational economic actors? Economics experiments show we are not. Understanding this opens us to other important questions to consider, such as, Is market behavior the only or best way to gauge preferences, or might we allow for thoughtful, patient introspection concerning the root causes of suffering and happiness? Does the market really offer an accurate and comprehensive valuation of community, or might we allow for forms of fellowship that elude economic objectification?

In economics as in other fields, the limitations of its methods are projected onto reality, truncating our image of self and community in ways that ultimately are not only wrong but pernicious. Real people and their lives disappear behind the equations, and the densely interconnected world in which we live is replaced by a more tractable limited system of competing individuals and corporations that produce and consume. Objectification and impersonal economic transactions come to not only dominate our models but also infect our views of each other and the natural world.

The failure of traditional economics to account for what are called "externalities" is a symptom of its tragic neglect of the interconnectedness we have been considering. For example, the additional health and environmental costs caused by the pollution associated with production are "externalized," which is to say they are not borne by manufacturers but by the populace and the environment. Impacts on the environment and community are obvious if one has a worldview that acknowledges the dense interconnections between human activity, environment, and health. Instead, classical economics neglects them. "Ecological economics" or "natural capitalism" is an emerging alternative to classical economics that explicitly rejects the way in which neoclassical theory treats externalities.[7]

The critique goes deeper. In his book *The Dismal Science*, Harvard professor of economics Stephen Marglin characterizes economics as "hobbled by an ideology in which these tensions [between individual and whole, between self-interest and obligation to others, between material and spiritual health] are replaced by a set of pseudo-universals about human nature."[8] Doing so simplifies the modeling but at great cost. Marglin goes on to provide a foundational critique that reaches beyond the inclusion of externalities to the very ways in which community—necessary to a good life—is systematically undermined by markets that replace personal ties with impersonal market transactions. He shows that the effects of this process on well-being and the quality of life are large and negative.

Further problems arise in economics because of its impoverished view of the human being. Two examples will help make clear what I mean. The first is the Ultimatum Game, which economic researchers are now using to explore the limits of the basic assumptions of neoclassical economics, those assumptions being that *homo economicus* always acts rationally and in his or her own self-interest.[9] In this model, emotions, altruism, fairness, community, and so on have no real place in the economic calculations. In the Ultimatum Game I receive a day's wages from someone with the condition that I give you some portion of what I received. If you keep the portion I give you, then the division of money between us is settled. If you

83

do not keep the portion given, then both of us forfeit the money. According to standard economic calculations, since something is always better than nothing, you will keep whatever amount I give you, otherwise you (and I) lose the money. Taking whatever is given is the rational, self-interested thing to do. Experiments show, however, that in all cultures if the amount given is below about 25 percent, you will refuse the offer. Irrational factors or violations of self-interest are at play.[10] Why are we not surprised by the result? Because we too would reject a demeaning offer, no matter what the economists say.

The second recognized failure of neo-economic theory is the "tragedy of the commons." Our survival as a species depends fundamentally on such common resources as air that is suitable to breathe, water that can be drunk, fish in the sea, soil that will grow crops, and so on. But if fishermen, farmers, and other workers act rationally and purely in their self-interest, then the neoclassical economic calculation predicts the collapse of fish stocks, the disappearance of water, and so on. Without someone acting on behalf of everyone, without a selfless sense for the whole, the tragedy of the commons will take place. But societies do step back and regulate fishing, water rights, and air quality on behalf of the community and future generations. Such acts as these are not part of the traditional economic calculus. The significance of this failure was recently underscored by the Nobel Prize committee when they awarded the 2009 Nobel Prize in Economics to Elinor Ostrom for her work on the tragedy of the commons.

With these and other groundbreaking economic studies in behavioral economics, wellness studies, and game theory, we are beginning to see the incursion of a more phenomenological and nonreductive approach to the understanding of people's economic life. Through these approaches the actual economic behavior of human beings is studied instead of presumed or idealized behavior. These are complemented by psychological and neuroscientific studies, which are also opening new ways of thinking about economics.

Enlarging our view of the human being and enriching our relations to the world we inhabit will change not only the content of our courses but our pedagogy as well. Three examples can stand for many. At the University of Southern Maine, professor of economics Vaishali Mamgain offers a course on neoclassical economics and happiness in which she not only reviews research on this topic but asks her students to work reflectively with questions such as these:

- What are the causes and conditions that make you happy?
- Who is it that is experiencing happiness?
- Are happiness and pleasure the same thing?

Political philosopher David Kahane at the University of Alberta draws his students into the deep moral issues around allocation of resources by asking students to examine their own choices. With great sensitivity, he then invites them to view in a sustained way the image of an African mother burying her child who has died from an entirely preventable illness. Kahane notes that the cost of a latté is equal to rehydration therapy for five children. Both Mamgain and Kahane seek to join textbook material with the experiences and inner observations of their students. Students are explicitly asked to bring themselves into the material and to offer thoughtful comments based on introspection.

Frank Maddox is an award-winning economics professor at Oxford College of Emory University who teaches in a similar way. He uses a variety of strategies to make vivid the realities of poverty and wealth, industrial and craft production, and consumption. For instance, after his students have studied standard economic theory in which consumers are modeled as maximizing utility, he gives them an unusual assignment. They are asked to go to a store like Wal-Mart or McDonald's and note the expressions, actions, and so on of the people there. Students are to observe, without judgment, anything that will help them gauge the degree of consciousness shoppers give to what they are doing. Then Maddox asks the students to observe themselves in the same way, again without judgment. How attentive are they to what they are doing at any moment? What would it mean for us if we were more aware of our consumption? He calls it mindful consumption, and he asks what it might mean to replace maximizing utility with mindful consumption. At the end of the semester Maddox's economics students all present their Interbeing Projects. *Interbeing* is a term taken from the Buddhist teacher Thich Nhat Hanh that emphasizes the interconnectedness of all things. Students select a consumer good or service and then research some aspect of its production, becoming more conscious of their connections and responsibilities to it. Maddox teaches economics not only with interconnectedness in mind but as an experience for his students.

In the same vein, author Daniel Goleman in his book *Ecological Intelligence* makes a compelling case for the huge environmental and social benefits that would occur if we practiced mindful consumption, especially when the technologies become available to support us in this practice at the point of purchase.[11] For example, in an early version of such a technology, the foundation Nature & More rates hundreds of products and profiles producers and their social and environmental practices, all available on its website.

As the second example of the benefits of the relational and integrative view of reality, consider health care and medical education. In the United States, our approach to medicine has increasingly become a reductive science married to a for-profit economic model that is fast approaching collapse. The questions of the quality of care for the whole person and the education of the whole physician seldom rise to the top of the agenda. Instead, cost analyses and technique pervade the system and threaten to overwhelm the idealistic motives that draw most medical and nursing students to the profession. At every step, caring for those who are ill and suffering is made increasingly difficult by a system at odds with itself. I hardly need describe the dangers of a truncated biomedical model that sees the human being purely as a collection of organs, blood levels, and test results. Good medical education and health care does not require such a view; in fact, it seems obvious that a fully integrative view is called for.

For several years I taught an interdisciplinary course that studied, among other topics, the human body in art and science. We worked equally with the anatomical drawings of Leonardo da Vinci and the scientific study of the heart by Andreas Vesalius

86

and William Harvey. The capstone experience was a trip to the anatomy lab of the University of Massachusetts Medical School in Worcester, which was run by the remarkable teacher and anatomist Sandy Marks. When Marks first began teaching, anatomy classes had historically been taught as a grisly, even macabre, boot-camp experience. Early on he noted that some of his best students were dropping out of medical school as a result. His own sensibilities, as well as conversations with students in his class, led him to a total overhaul of the gross anatomy class.

Now the first day of class begins with readings and conversations about death. For many students the cadaver they will dissect is their first direct encounter with mortality. It often raises fears and memories of those they have lost. Marks makes time and space for these recollections and feelings. He then introduces the students to their "first patient." No longer taken from the state's unclaimed dead, each body has been donated to the medical school, some coming with personal letters or poems expressing the wishes of the deceased. He read one to us: "May that life force that ran in me shine forth once more and pass to you the knowledge and the power that help sustain the miracle of life."[12] In this class, each medical student takes the body apart layer by layer, learning its miracles, but now it is done with respect and ever mindful of the gift. At the conclusion of the class, relatives of the deceased are invited to a closing ceremony in the medical school courtyard at which the students express in words, music, and poetry their deep gratitude for the gift of the body they studied.

Sandy Marks passed away in 2002. The last group of students he taught composed and read this poem at his memorial service:[13]

I sat in tears and you told me about dying.
I watched in horror as you took the death from another's body.
I lost myself on my way to your office, but when I got there,
    you had found me.
Knowledge, you offered us.
Humor, you provided for us.
Humanity, you required of us.
Stability, you granted us.

Instant, unwavering stability.
We watched, listened, spoke, heard,
    laughed, feared, cried,
    refused, overcame, denied,
    and responded.
And with a wink and a nudge of your elbow, you calmed the
    eruption of emotional chaos.
We learned.
And with a wink and a nudge of your elbow, you made it
    clear why.

— NICOLE LEBOEUF, UMMS CLASS OF 2006

Our day at the anatomy lab recapitulated in miniature the medical school experience, from the meeting with death and dissection to the conversations about loss and love. It was an amazing and moving experience for our Amherst College students, one they never forgot. They experienced a profoundly ethical form of education in which knowing and caring were united.

In pedagogies of experience and interconnections, we are often challenged by the worldview and values of those we meet. Those we meet can think, feel, and act so differently than we do. Such experiences awaken us to our own culture, mores, and behavior, and this is especially so when our engagement with other communities is in service to them. In response to a request from us, Alma Blount describes an educational program that connects communities and the classroom in important ways. Working with people who hold conflicting values in a democratic society brings the realities of leadership and politics to life. Service Opportunities in Leadership (SOL), sponsored by the Hart Leadership Program in the Terry Sanford Institute of Public Policy at Duke University, is an intensive yearlong program for undergraduates that combines academic study, service to communities, and critical reflection. In writing about the program, Blount asks her students rhetorically,

What are the highest goals of this class? Informed by
scholarship and the ideas of your classmates, you will arm

yourself emotionally and intellectually to enter a new culture prepared to serve and to reflect critically on your experience there. We will ask you to think deeply about how to approach the inevitable value conflicts you will face as you cross the borders of new organizations and cultures. We will ask you to examine your own religious and cultural values and preconceptions. We will challenge you to explore how you can, over time, become a fully engaged citizen of your own society.

Alma Blount's effort is another example of how we can deepen learning in the classroom through experiences beyond its walls. (Her full text appears in Appendix A.)

INTERDISCIPLINARITY AND INTENTIONAL TEACHING

We can choose the way we teach. The teachers profiled in this chapter have each sought ways to give body and soul to the otherwise abstract concepts and depersonalized practices of their discipline. They have sought ways of inviting students to make use of their own experiences by pausing to quietly question, reflect, feel, and write. As the students go on to become engaged citizens, doctors, economists, and even consumers, that habit of pausing, reflecting, honoring, and acting morally will serve them and our society.

Sandy Marks and his students reformed their anatomy lesson, making the laboratory at once an educational and a sacred space that welcomed all of who they were: body, mind, and spirit. Might we not do likewise? When we do, the ripples are likely to go far beyond our individual classrooms. Is it any accident that Jon Kabat-Zinn began his revolutionary work in mindfulness-based stress reduction down the hall from Sandy Marks? Every bold integrative initiative in higher education will find its echo because we are in the company of others who will respond in their own unique way to our honest efforts at cultivating humanity.

In recent decades another way of striving to innovate in higher education has been through efforts at interdisciplinary teaching

Attending to Interconnection, Living the Lesson

and research. Those involved have sought to bring disparate areas of learning together to illuminate each other, and much has been gained in the process. I have relished the many interdisciplinary courses I have taught over thirty years with colleagues from across the campus: Romanticism and the Enlightenment, The Imagined Landscape, Eros and Insight, to name a few. These courses brought me together with brilliant scholar-teachers from whom I learned and was enriched. In such classes students saw firsthand the ways in which every issue begs to be addressed from multiple directions. Few issues are adequately treated from a single disciplinary perspective, and the lively engagement of two or more colleagues who tackle an issue, text, or historical period demonstrates this truism again and again.

While interdisciplinary teaching brings much to learning, it is not by itself necessarily truly integrative. Most often it is a case of simple juxtaposition. The scholars each bring their expertise and place their contribution beside that of their colleagues. The students are left with the difficult task of synthesizing the parts into a whole on their own. For these classes to be truly integrative, faculty need to exemplify integrative understanding through the ways in which they connect diverse fields into a comprehensive integrated whole.

For example, Princeton psychologist Daniel Kahneman was awarded the 2002 Nobel Prize in Economics for his development of prospect theory, which concerns decision making in the face of risk. Kahneman made a seminal contribution to economic theory without ever taking a single course in the field of economics. He and his colleagues worked across disciplinary boundaries, bringing psychology and economics into a profoundly fruitful integration. Harvard Nobel economist Amartya Sen has reached out the other way to include a very wide range of non-economic factors into his economic analysis, including individual and societal values, human development, and the rights of individuals. Originality does not respect disciplinary divisions.

Each semester students take courses across the curriculum, especially if they are in liberal arts colleges, that support a broad-based education. They should be encouraged to bring all of who they are and what they know into each class. When in a literature class studying, for example, Keats's conception of "negative capability" ("when man is capable of being in uncertainties, mysteries, doubts without any irritable reaching after fact & reason"[14]), students might well draw on understandings and experiences of this capacity from areas as diverse as psychology, religious studies, quantum logic, and Gödel's incompleteness theorem. Poets are not the only ones who deal in uncertainties, mysteries, and doubts. With this simple realignment, we shift our focus from the technical understanding of a literary reference to students' whole learning; we thereby become interested in students in their entirety not merely as budding literary scholars. Cross-disciplinary initiatives are needed if we are to prepare our students to meet the real problems our society faces. No one field has all the answers because real issues possess multiple dimensions.

By welcoming the *whole* student into our classes, unfamiliar aspects of who they are and what they care about suddenly come into view. What are the heartfelt questions they struggle with? Are they too scared to acknowledge the hopes and aspirations they harbor for their lives and for this world? If they fail to voice them in the safety of a college classroom, will they ever dare to live their aspirations later? And what if we would reciprocate by revealing unfamiliar aspects of ourselves? Too often we hide in our specializations when, in fact, our interests, experiences, hopes, and understandings are far broader than we let on. In brief, we should do far more to support both students and faculty who strive to combine depth of knowledge in a special area with breath and integration. Working with such contradictory intellectual gestures may well be the hallmark of great innovation, and our pedagogies should strive to foster the capacity to sustain and use contradictions to their fullest.

The solitude of specialization often reflects a wider disconnection from others. Classroom culture reinforces that disconnection, not only between teacher and student but also between students. Patricia Owen-Smith wondered why "life in the academy has been consistently alienating and lonely" for her. (For Owen-Smith's full text, see Appendix A.) Gradually she came "to understand that the academic world of higher education has been structured in

Attending to Interconnection, Living the Lesson

such a way so as to normalize and promote alienation. Under the guise of academic freedom and professional autonomy we close our classroom and office doors physically and metaphorically." Upon realizing this, Owen-Smith set about changing the culture of her classroom. In her case, she introduced a period of listening to music at the start of each class, with the encouragement to be still and to "go within." She felt awkward at first, but slowly the students warmed to the innovation, bringing in their own music and appreciating the time of stillness and the journey within. In her description for us, Owen-Smith writes:

> As we neared the end of the semester the structure of the class had changed from a group of individuals reluctantly gathered together for study to a community of friends and partners who were creating a space of introspection, quiet, and respect for the process of study and the development of self.... It has been a decade since this initial introduction of contemplative music and I cannot envision a classroom without music. Semester after semester, I watch with delight as we take a journey together, a journey whereby we hear our souls, breathe in silence, cherish stillness, and learn from one another in the most enduring ways. Our journey is a dance, a conversation, a celebration of the heart, and a sacred moment in the process we call "education."

With each additional view of a landscape, we enrich our appreciation of its character and beauty. With each added intimacy, we come to know a person better and more fully. No one view contains the whole truth, but by moving among and between a myriad of them we may gain an intimation of a truth which lies forever beyond our grasp. Such is the living work of integrative teaching and learning to which the university in its entirety should be dedicated.

Such synthetic efforts need to be supported within our universities and colleges. Yet if they are truly integrative, they may well be contrary to the traditional departmental structure of the academy, whose power and reluctance to change we should not underestimate. Much would be gained by fostering a university culture that simultaneously values disciplinary specialization and truly integrative research and teaching. That is, while we rightly value the specialized knowledge of each separate discipline, we should give encouragement to scholars who step outside their specialization to integrate novel areas into their research and teaching. To this end, we need to find ways to promote conversations around issues that draw together diverse voices, viewpoints, and competencies. We recognize that starting such conversations requires boldness, and we offer suggestions on how to begin these kinds of conversations in Chapter 6.

Enriching Epistemology, Fostering Imagination

The wish to comprehend leads us to develop methods of inquiry directed toward reliable knowledge. If the methods we possess are fragmentary or partial, then our knowledge will be likewise. In this way we see that an expanded ontology requires an enriched epistemology. The richness of the world will not reveal itself by a single means of inquiry. Not only are many questions required, but they must be posed and explored in different ways, each one of which illuminates the world from another direction, inner as well as outer.

Let us return to and dwell a little longer on the illusive human capacity of imagination so central to a vital and genuine university. Ralph Waldo Emerson described imagination as profoundly participatory: a knowing by becoming. "Imagination," he wrote, "is a very high sort of seeing, which does not come by study, but by the intellect being where and what it sees."[15] The intellect of the inquiring individual shifts the locus of its activity from itself into the other. Through imagination, the mind finds a way of living for a time beyond itself, becoming "where and what it sees." As Palmer has already mentioned, Evelyn Fox Keller characterized biologist Barbara McClintock's method as "learning by identification" so that the object she was studying (maize) became a subject.[16]

Attending to Interconnection, Living the Lesson

The epistemology of imagination rejects objectification and distancing and instead practices what we might term subjectification and intimacy. This is McClintock's "intimacy that does not annihilate difference." It is a patient, contemplative method that seeks "to hear what the material has to say to you," and through which one achieves "a feeling for the organism." In an address to young Harvard biology students, McClintock urged them to "take the time and look," but as her biographer Keller rightly commented, today "the pace of research seems to preclude such a contemplative stance." Yet it is precisely this contemplative stance that is essential to an integrative and imaginative education within our contemporary culture of teaching and learning.

For these reasons I view the practice of *contemplative inquiry* as an essential modality of study complementary to the dominant analytic methods now practiced in every field.[17] I see contemplative inquiry as the expression of an *epistemology of love* that is the true heart of higher education. *Epistemology* means "theory of knowledge," or how we know what we know. At first, love seems to have little to do with knowledge and our understanding of how it works, but if we set aside romantic love for the moment, is it not true that we come to know best that which we love most? To make this method clearer, I will distinguish seven stages in the epistemology of love.

The first stage is *respect*. We cannot take the ethical orientation of research for granted. We should consciously adopt a positive ethical orientation toward our object of study. What is the quality and character of our interest in what lies before us? Do we respect the integrity of the other, be it a poem, a plant, or a patient? In his *Letters to a Young Poet*, Rilke suggested that the highest we can offer another is to "stand guard over their solitude."[18] When we truly respect the integrity of the other, we "border and protect" them, Rilke suggested, even while we seek to know them more completely.

The second stage is *gentleness*. In his own scientific investigations, the poet Goethe, like McClintock, sought to practice what he called a "gentle empiricism [*zarte Empirie*]."[19] If we wish to approach the object of our attention without distorting it, then we must be gentle. By contrast, the empiricism of Francis Bacon spoke

THE HEART OF HIGHER EDUCATION

of extracting nature's secrets under extreme conditions, of putting her to the rack. An epistemology of love rejects such methods.

The third stage is *intimacy*. Conventional science distances itself from nature and, to use Erwin Schrödinger's term, *objectifies* nature.[20] Under this view, science disengages itself from phenomena for the sake of objectivity. Contemplative inquiry, by contrast, approaches the phenomenon delicately and respectfully, but it does nonetheless seek to become intimate with that to which it attends. We can still retain clarity and balanced judgment close-up, if we remember to exercise restraint and gentleness. The new science makes clear the implications of such intimacy in its account of observation.

The fourth stage is *vulnerability*. In order to know, we must open ourselves to the other. In order to move with and be influenced by the other, we must be confident enough to be vulnerable, secure enough to open ourselves to the being and becoming of the unknown. A dominating arrogance will not serve. We must learn to be comfortable with *not* knowing, with ambiguity and uncertainty. Only from what may appear to be weakness and ignorance can the new arise.

The fifth stage is *participation*. Gentle and vulnerable intimacy leads to participation in the unfolding phenomenon before us. Outer characteristics invite us to go deeper. We move and feel with the natural phenomenon, text, painting, or person before us, living out of ourselves and into the other. Respectfully and delicately, we join with the other, while maintaining full awareness and clarity of mind. In other words, an epistemology of love is experientially centered in the other, not in ourselves. In Emerson's language "the intellect being where and what it sees." Our usual preoccupations, fears, and cravings work against authentic participation.

The sixth stage is *transformation*. The last two characteristics, participation and vulnerability, lead to a patterning of ourselves on the other. What was outside us is now internalized. Inwardly we assume the shape, dynamic, and meaning of the contemplated object. We are, in a word, transformed by experience in accord with the object of contemplation. The individual is developed, or we could say is sculpted, through the above practices.

95

The lineage of education as transformation dates back to at least as far as the Greeks. In his book *What Is Ancient Philosophy?* the French philosopher Pierre Hadot writes that for the ancient philosopher, "the goal was to develop a *habitus*, or new capacity to judge or criticize, and to transform—that is, to change people's way of living and seeing the world."[21] Simplicius asked, "What place shall the philosopher occupy in the city? That of a sculptor of men." Or as Merleau-Ponty has put it, we need to relearn how to see the world.[22] In an essay on science, Goethe gave voice to a potent pedagogical principle: "Every object well-contemplated opens a new organ of perception in us."[23] Echoing Goethe's view while commenting on McClintock, Evelyn Fox Keller remarks that "a motivated observer develops faculties that a casual spectator may never be aware of."[24] The innate capacities for imaginative cognition that are everyone's common inheritance are animated and developed through the patient practice of an epistemology of love.

The seventh stage is *imaginative insight.* The ultimate result of contemplative engagement as outlined here is, as Goethe might have called it, organ formation, which leads in turn to imaginative insight born of an intimate participation in the course of things. In Buddhist epistemology this has been called "direct perception"; among the Greeks it was called *episteme* and was contrasted to inferential reasoning. Knowing of this type is experienced as a kind of seeing, beholding, or direct apprehension, rather than as an intellectual reasoning to a logical conclusion.[25] It is the moment of creative insight which every scientist, scholar, and artist recognizes as the axis around which their work turns but which cannot be produced on demand. Simone Weil termed it "grace."[26] In his journal Emerson conjoins artistic and scientific creativity by the illuminating remark, "Never did any science originate, but by a poetic perception."[27]

While insight is the guide of wise action, its accomplishment requires restraint. We must pause to reflect before speaking, quietly engage the issue inwardly before acting, open ourselves to not-knowing before certainty arises, and so we live for a time in the question before the answer emerges. Only under such conditions can the imagination work; recall Keats's negative capability. In "East Coker" T. S. Eliot describes the need for open awareness without expectation: "Or when under ether, the mind is conscious but conscious of nothing—/ I said to my soul, be still, and wait without hope." Poetry, indeed all art as well as all science, flows from such restraint.

In a paper written during her first year at Amherst College, Annie Handler struggled to hold the tension between knowing and loving that resolves itself in an epistemology of love. Already at eighteen Annie longed to learn, longed to embrace equally both the sciences and the arts. In her final paper for the first-year seminar Eros and Insight, she wrote:

> This true nourishment of the mind and body is often mistaken
> with a false nourishment of material objects; however, when
> looking at Marguerite Porete's words "love Love and do as you
> will" it is clear that the true nourishment of life and living is a
> love of knowledge—knowledge of the arts and sciences. No
> other nourishment is as capable of sustaining life as these two,
> for the fusion of knowledge and passion for the arts and
> sciences ultimately lead to a state of immortality, and as
> Diotima reveals [in Plato's *Symposium*], reaching a state of
> immortality is a state for which all humans aspire.

Annie has worked as an intern in the National Institutes of Health for the last four summers doing research on Parkinson's disease and the brain. And yet she refuses to isolate the science she does from the art she loves. In a recent e-mail to me, she wrote, "Eros & Insight has given me the greatest gift any science researcher could ask for—the perspective that allows me to simultaneously see the art in nature and the possibilities for incorporating that art into the research of science."

So, we come full circle. What began in respectful wonder flows back as insightful and harmonious action in the world and human society. Modestly, we recognize that our knowledge is a reflection of our means of inquiry and the context of our question, and we realize

Attending to Interconnection, Living the Lesson

that by attentively circling our subject we enrich our understanding. Traditionally distinct disciplines begin to interweave. Confronted by the problems of the environment, we weave together the insights of science, economics, politics, communication, and even the arts. Each contributes to the fullness of our understanding and the pragmatics of action. Expanding our ontology and enriching our epistemologies in the ways I have indicated is, in my view, a requirement for any future philosophy of education that will give us the integrative education our students and our world sorely need.

Awakening Compassion

As Parker Palmer rightly observed, the final crucial stone in the infrastructure of integrative education derives from the principle, "Every epistemology, or way of knowing, as implemented in a pedagogy, or way of teaching and learning, tends to become an ethic, or way of living." We believe that ethical thinking and action are supported by integrative teaching and learning. Compassionate action is fostered in students when they learn not only with the intellect but also with the heart. As I have attempted to show, an epistemology of love bridges the divide between intellect and feelings, between objectivity and participation. Once knowing activates our feelings, we are moved to action. We move from being a bystander to being a neighbor or friend. Our intimate understanding of others and their needs prompts compassionate action.

We find an instance of exactly this in the program initiated by Judy Goodell and Joan Avis from the University of San Francisco. (For a full description of this program, see Appendix B.) They note that like so many other universities with noble mission statements, "the motto of USF is 'educating hearts and minds to change the world.'" Putting these fine words into action, Goodell, Avis, and their students started an educational initiative in the Mayan town of Tekit in the Yucatán which sought to support the education of Mayan youth through high school. As they describe it,

The program was designed to meet the educational needs and development of the whole person. We believed from the outset that education of the mind, heart, and spirit must unfold concurrently for meaningful change to occur. Yet even we were amazed at what began to take shape as teachers and learners opened themselves to deep engagement in the circles of each other's lives.

Through their description of the project, one senses the pedagogical power that helping others brings with it. Words like *meaning*, *values*, and *purpose* lose their abstract philosophical ring when we are aiding others. The capacities we have cultivated are finally put to real, ethical use, and we are motivated to learn more and become more human for the sake of others. Such engagement is one of mutual benefit; an ethical action, rightly taken, invites a reciprocal generosity that can appear in unexpected ways. Integrative education embodies the principle of reciprocity. In the words of Goodell and Avis,

> Delivering an integrative educational program in a different culture requires a willingness to participate in community ritual events and story making; it is with curiosity, joy, and gratitude that we have done so. It is part of the rich legacy of our own learning. Integrative participatory education is reciprocal. When one heart, mind, and spirit connects to another, both become teacher and learner, and both are changed.

Chapter 5

Experience, Contemplation, and Transformation

Arthur Zajonc

One of the neglected dimensions of our educational system concerns the transformative power true education possesses. Even after many decades of research and writing on developmental psychology, neuroplasticity, and the intersubjective formation of consciousness, we seldom incorporate the results of such research into our teaching. Our institutions of higher education seldom embrace a genuinely transformative view of the pedagogies they consciously, or more often unconsciously, adopt. Our view of the student is too often as a vessel to be filled or a person to be trained. Is this so surprising? A diminished anthropology is a natural corollary to our diminished ontology.

We need, therefore, to become more attentive to our students' intellectual, emotional, and character development and learn to see them as richly endowed, malleable beings open to cognitive and affective changes through pedagogical interventions and social formation. We should attend to the cultivation of our students' humanity at least as much as we instruct them in the content of our fields. In this way higher education, both in the classroom and beyond, can balance its informative task with transformation, which is of equal or greater importance. Long after they forget the content they learned, who they have become will endure and determine much of the character and quality of their contribution to society and the personal satisfaction they take in life.

True integrative higher education must, therefore, make use of the extensive investigation of and insights into the stages of cognitive, affective, moral, and spiritual development of the human being throughout life as articulated by such researchers as William Perry, Jack Mezirow, Robert Kegan, Lawrence Kohlberg, Sharon Parks, and Ken Wilber.[1] Each of these has argued that in addition to the acquisition of knowledge and skills, children and adults also mature through stages each one of which changes the fundamental way in which they make meaning of the world. Mezirow terms these transformations of "perspective" or later "frames of reference"; Kegan calls them changes in our epistemologies. These researchers suggest that a developmental or transformative approach is the most powerful way to conceptualize the growth of the whole human being, and that growth should also be an important goal of higher education. In all cases a simple model of education that is exclusively viewed as a process of information transfer, mastery, and application is shown to be inadequate.

Modern neuroscience has enabled us to understand, at least in part, the neurological correlates of psychological development. During the early years, much of a child's neurological development is genetically driven and unfolds according to an innate timetable.[2] Additionally, the environment is a powerful force in the formative years of childhood, working strongly on the nervous system. One can gear pedagogy during those years to match the neurological developmental stages of childhood. But even when the nervous system is developed fully in late adolescence, research has shown that it remains surprisingly plastic and therefore open to continued transformation and further development through conscious schooling.[3] Research on violinists, London cab drivers, and others has demonstrated that dramatic shifting of mental resources and the growth of neural connections is associated with practice and schooling. Recall Goethe's refrain, "Every object, well-contemplated, opens a new organ in us." Goethe's maxim and Mezirow's vision of transformative education are receiving more and more support from the fast-paced research in cognitive and affective neurosciences.

In researching the epistemologies we use throughout life, Robert Kegan has identified six stages (labeled 0–5), the last three of which concern the adult learner. By the time of university schooling the learner has most likely attained what Kegan calls "the Socialized Mind." At this point, she has sufficiently internalized the cognitive structures, aesthetics, customs, mores, and expectations of her culture such that her thoughts and actions naturally reflect the internalized epistemological and moral system she needs to make meaning of the world. In a conventional sense, such students are well-adjusted, and have an easy time with the norms and traditional knowledge of their society, but their development is incomplete.

The next stage is the Self-Authoring Mind, in which the individual can internalize divergent points of view and author his or her own independent one. Kegan's own longitudinal studies as well as those of others indicate that "around one-half to two-thirds of the adult population appears not to have fully reached the fourth order of consciousness."[4] Thus, university education usually means helping the student to move from stage three (the Socialized Mind) to stage four (the Self-Authoring Mind). King and Baxter Magolda go so far as to declare, "The achievement of self-authorship (Kegan's level 4) should be heralded as a central purpose of higher education."[5] The task of university learning is thus most often to challenge the generally unconscious cognitive structures and moral habits associated with the Socialized Mind and to encourage the development of the new epistemological framework provided by the Self-Authoring Mind. In Kegan's view, during the college years the teacher works with the student to build "developmental bridges" from one epistemological stage to another. Challenging a widely held, unconscious assumption can lead to animated class engagement that, if sustained and developed, may be one of the key components in constructing a developmental bridge to a new epistemology or order of consciousness.

The fifth and final order of consciousness Kegan terms "the Self-Transforming Mind." It is characterized by the release of the individualized viewpoint and the sustaining of multiple dynamically changing and even contradictory viewpoints at the same time. Kegan describes it as granting one the possibility for

> the recognition of our multiple selves, for the capacity to see conflict as an over-identification with a single system, for the sense of our relationships and connections as prior to and constitutive of the individual self, for an identification with the transformative process of our being rather than the formative products of our becoming.[6]

In all his research, Kegan has encountered a mere handful of adults who are at this order of consciousness.

To this can be added research in the area of social and emotional intelligence that has demonstrated the powerful role of empathy in the intersubjective development of human consciousness.[7] Research points us to the fact that we learn best through our relationships. As Daniel Goleman writes in his comprehensive account of the social foundations of intelligence, we are "hardwired" for social learning, imitating down to the level of neurons what is occurring around us.[8] Such imitation is formative, shaping the very cognitive, emotional, and moral faculties we use to make sense of the world. The lessons of social and emotional learning should not be lost on adult educators. Learning communities that emphasize group work and sustained collaboration harness the reality of social foundations of learning. Again, the transformative as well as the informative dimensions of social intelligence are crucial here.

PEDAGOGIES OF TRANSFORMATION

Most conventional methods of instruction are too weak and fragmented to affect a significant shift in perspective, epistemology, or moral level of the type envisioned by Kegan, Mezirow, Kohlberg, and others. Transformative thinkers hold that a more intense, sustained, active, and experiential modality of engagement is required in order to effect the deeper changes required for a new way of making meaning. When Turiel observed the effect of children passively listening to the moral views of adults concerning ethical dilemmas, he found that the changes in the children's own moral judgments were slight.[9] Changing our way of making meaning of a complex world requires a paradigm shift analogous to the shift from a geocentric to a heliocentric worldview. The outer facts of life may be the same, but their significance to us and the actions that follow change dramatically in the wake of such a shift.[10]

Such deep changes take time; a single class period will not do the trick. We evolve slowly into the new paradigm or frame of reference. Rilke's advice to the young poet Franz Kappus is apt in this regard.

> I would like to beg you dear Sir, as well as I can, to have
> patience with everything unresolved in your heart and to try to
> cherish the questions themselves as if they were closed rooms or
> books written in a very strange tongue. Do not search now for
> the answers, which could not be given to you because you would
> not be able to live them. It is a matter of living everything. Live
> the questions now. Perhaps you will then gradually, without
> noticing it, one distant day live right into the answer.[11]

By lovingly holding the questions themselves, contemplating them well, we gradually, without noticing it, develop faculties of insight ("organs," Goethe might say) that allow us to see and live the answers. Perhaps surprisingly, *theory* derives from the Greek word meaning "to behold." Living our way into the answers means to so change ourselves that we are capable of beholding and inhabiting a different world. The demands of that new world may well be great.

Experience, Contemplation, and Transformation

In Kohlberg's theory of moral stage development, for example, "postconventional" moral principles may be at odds with the conventional ethical and legal standards of the community of which one is a part. A Mahatma Gandhi, Martin Luther King, or Nelson Mandela will stand up to the unjust laws of an oppressive regime, but most of us go along with the prevailing conventional social norms and comply with tradition. Even today the caste system of India, racism in the United States, and ethnic biases around the world are difficult to overcome in large part because the powerful forces that shape conventional morality are rooted in tradition, which have become internalized into the very ways people make meaning. It orders their world, even if tragically so.

In order to change, we must first find ways to temporarily inhabit other ways of being and knowing, exploring them for a time, trying alternatives on for size. Therefore, a prerequisite for an enduring shift in meaning making is that we are able to place ourselves in the world of others. Empathetic and imaginative knowing does exactly this; we repeatedly live others' lives, experience their joys and sorrows, their trials and successes.

Literature, history, philosophy, indeed every field offers students the opportunity for a form of imaginative exploration, whether it be of an unfamiliar culture, a new human dilemma, or the baffling properties of non-Euclidean geometry. It is this exploration that leads to change. The moral admonition "discrimination is wrong" changes nothing in us. But truly "living the question" empathetically and imaginatively does change us and the way we make intellectual and moral meaning of our world. In this way we learn by becoming another, giving up one perspective for a different one. Such empathetic and imaginative experiences can drive the transformation of the individual from the Socialized Mind to the Self-Authoring Mind and perhaps even beyond that to the Self-Transforming Mind. In each case the subsequent epistemology is more self-conscious and encompassing than the former.

When Goethe writes of a "delicate empiricism," I believe he has in mind this kind of transformation of the self in which a new

THE HEART OF HIGHER EDUCATION

way of seeing becomes possible. It requires a deep identification with the object and an empathetic understanding:

> There is a delicate empiricism that makes itself utterly identical with the object, thereby becoming true theory. But this enhancement of our mental powers belongs to a highly evolved age.[12]

The "enhancement of our mental powers" of which Goethe writes is essential to education. Goethe could be describing the marvels of recent research on neuroplasticity when, in a letter to F. H. Jacobi, he wrote,

> To grasp the phenomena, to fix them to experiments, to arrange the experiences and know the possible modes of representation of them .... demands a molding of man's poor ego, a transformation so great that I never should have believed it possible.[13]

Transformative learning rests on an enriched view of the human being, one that affirms our multidimensional nature and fundamental malleability. The methods by which we challenge our students, open them to change, will vary, but to be successful they should include cross-cultural studies in which worldviews radically different from their own are encountered and appreciated. Or one can look back sympathetically at other historical periods and the surprisingly different treatment given to social issues or natural phenomena. Finally, cognitive science and psychology are also rich with empirical studies that awaken us to the unconscious cognitive or moral processes underlying our judgments and actions.

Artists understand the central importance of transformative learning well. In a 1904 letter to Emil Bernard, Paul Cézanne wrote: "There is only nature, and the eye is trained through contact with her. It becomes concentric through looking and working."[14] That is to say, we start eccentric to nature, off-center. Through our constant attention to her we become concentric; we reshape ourselves with

Experience, Contemplation, and Transformation

every stroke on the canvas to be in alignment with her. Only in this way does the artist learn to see the as-yet-unseen and so become capable of rendering it visible to others.

EXPERIENTIAL LEARNING

Much has been made of experiential learning, but its real significance becomes evident within a comprehensive view of an expanded ontology and an enriched epistemology as discussed in the previous chapters. In these discussions, I've argued that the ontological standing of experience be elevated from mere secondary appearance to a central position in our new phenomenological orientation. We are most powerfully affected by deep and sustained experiences, which leave enduring imprints on our very constitution and consciousness. We not only know more but see differently and become another human being through transformative experiences.

Experiential learning is most often associated with special occasions, often off-campus experiences in service, which are then the object of group conversation and reflection. Many colleges and universities have centers for community engagement that facilitate experiential and service learning. By offering students formal opportunities to pursue experiential learning in college, we give them the chance to live life's great questions in real time, to witness the struggles of others, to struggle themselves, and to form ethical positions in the face of life's genuine moral dilemmas. From recent research we can now appreciate how significant reflection is for the integration of experience into the student's learning, and how beneficial it is to connect the service component to a corresponding course. Experience alone opens a door, but intellectual framing and reflection are required if meaning is to be made of the experience.

For example, one day a student, Rachel, walked into Marshall Eakin's office at Vanderbilt University. In his report to us concerning the meeting and its consequences, Eakin movingly describes how his own reluctance to work with Rachel gradually changed into a partnership and a service-learning project in Chile, which has grown to include other countries and many more students since its inception. (For the full text of Eakin's description, see Appendix B.) His experience shows beautifully how a conversation with a student can become the impetus for curricular and pedagogical innovation. As we will discuss later, true speaking and listening—genuine conversation—is the rich source for much of the change we seek in higher education. In this case a conversation leads to a series of service-learning courses of great power through which ideas become grounded in lived experience. Eakin concludes his description with these words.

> My experience in service learning has made me a more committed and effective teacher. It has fundamentally redirected my teaching and my research—all of this due to the inspiration from Rachel and other students. Rachel's profound belief in the need to serve has inspired me since I met her, and continues to inspire me still. I am so lucky she walked into my office that spring day.

Given the widespread use of service learning at our colleges and universities, Marshall Eakin's story could be multiplied many times over. And we are now in a position to interpret his story and others against a unifying philosophical framework that values lived experience and reflection equally with critical reading and analysis. In addition, Eakin's emphasis on the inspiration he gained from a conversation with Rachel points to a key source of renewal in higher education.

Again and again one comes to appreciate the power of living the ideas about which one is lecturing. This was brought home to me through an experiential learning component of a course that took us to a residential community dedicated to the care of handicapped adults. The course, Re-Imagining the Human in a Technological Age, taught with art historian colleague Joel Upton, asked students to become conscious of the ways their habits of mind and the structure of their imagination shaped their experience of the world. In the first half of the course we moved them through the ways art and science had been differently shaped by the Gothic imagination,

Experience, Contemplation, and Transformation

the Renaissance imagination, and the Enlightenment, Romantic, and modern imaginations. At a certain point it became obvious to the students that, like those before them, they saw the world through a lens particular to their culture and upbringing. We then challenged them to re-imagine themselves and their world, to step outside the unconscious and comfortable habits of mind that so influenced their expectations, understandings, indeed their whole world. In order for them to appreciate the shift required we journeyed for a day to a community that decades ago had re-imagined what it meant to be profoundly mentally handicapped.

I have argued in this book that an essential dimension of higher education concerns the cultivation of our full humanity, but in what does that humanity consist? What does it take to be considered a person? Precisely here we are perhaps at the greatest peril if our ontology is too small. We may too quickly judge the nature and humanity of others by a shallow and limited set of criteria that does not allow for dimensions of the human being beyond intellect and physical fitness. In this way we not only distort our understanding of the precious being before us but also can be led to act inappropriately and even unethically toward him or her. (See, for example, the disturbing reasoning in Helga Kuhse and Peter Singer's *Should Baby Live? The Problem of Handicapped Infants.*[15])

Joel Upton and I took our students to a Camphill community populated by a hundred disabled adults who lived with over one hundred "normal" adults (called "coworkers") and children in large homelike settings on a beautiful 300-acre wooded campus. Long before "de-institutionalization," Camphill had created dozens of communities into which people with developmental and other disabilities could be completely integrated for life. During the day the disabled adults work side by side with the coworkers in craft shops making toys and candles, working the looms, and caring for the farm animals and large estate.[16] In the evenings they all return to their large home and share in all aspects of life. Camphill successfully re-imagined the life of the handicapped individual in community. Here was a living example of what it means to re-imagine one's world.

As part of our interdisciplinary course, each year late in the semester, we would clamber onto a bus in the early morning and depart Amherst College headed for Camphill. Even after the preparations we had given our students, I could always feel their anxiety at the prospect of meeting so many mentally disabled people. Most of our students had little or no experience with the disabled; their own lives had been ones of privilege and brilliance. The disabled were not part of their imagined or day-to-day community. What would it be like to spend the day working beside someone with severe disabilities, sharing meals and conversation?

As our bus pulled into the lovely rural campus of Camphill, we could see the "villagers" (as they are called) streaming out to meet us. Visitors are always a special treat. Some villagers were limping; all were grinning and waving a warm welcome. When my colleague and I stepped off the bus, we were immediately surrounded by a group of inquiring friends and acquaintances from our previous visits, and they peppered us with questions and embraced us. Our students descended from the bus hesitantly, but there was no hesitation on the side of the villagers. They took them in like familiar companions, asking them the same small set of questions they had asked us, pulling them along for a tea at the campus café before heading back to their workshops with their new charges. Within minutes the anxiety of our thirty Amherst students had disappeared and was replaced by wonder and openness to the day's adventure.

With our students divided up among their different disabled companions, I made my way to one house where a middle-aged friend with Down syndrome, a man I will call David, lived. My relation to David was special because his parents had died and his legal guardian (a dear friend of mine) had also died. Before my friend's death, he asked me to look in on David from time to time, which I gladly did. David was a very special, gentle, and loving person. He would dress up in a coat and tie for my every visit and take me to the barn on each occasion to show me the animals he cared for daily. He was one of the farmers, he would tell me with great pride, and indeed he was. While my students were working

111

and lunching with their village guides, I spent much of the day with David and, of course, his animals.

At the end of the afternoon, we assembled in the vaulted great hall of the community. Songs were sung, as best the villagers could—what was lacking in pitch was made up for with enthusiasm. Then questions from our students were posed to the leaders of the Camphill community. Much to their surprise, the leaders would turn to one or another of the villagers to have them answer each question no matter how complex or difficult, and the answers given were often so personal and vivid that one had difficulty maintaining composure. Their words might be poorly formed physically, but their views and heartfelt meaning were clear and moving. At the end of one visit, the villagers proudly told us the story of their performance not long before at Carnegie Hall. They described how they came out onto the great stage with their bells in hand at the end of a benefit concert by a stellar group of musicians. Before a visibly moved throng of New Yorkers, the Camphill bell choir played Pachelbel's Canon to much acclaim. They had had a great time, the villagers reported, and we should be sure to come to their next performance.

Through this experience, our students had lived for a moment into one example of *re-imagining* what it means to be human. They not only understood intellectually what it meant to re-imagine the human through historical examples; they also had experienced directly what it could mean for the lives of the disabled. And along the way they could ask, What does it mean to be human?

They also had an opportunity to understand what was important to them—and perhaps re-imagine their own world. More than once I heard a student say on the way back home, "Why couldn't Amherst be more like Camphill?" Indeed, why couldn't it?

CONTEMPLATIVE PEDAGOGY

The lessons of experiential learning in exceptional contexts can be learned in the ordinary classroom by making them more experiential. That is, we can ask, How can our engagement with the content of the class—whether poetry, physics, or anthropology—be made both more experiential and reflective? Over the years one method I and many others have used successfully in teaching has been the inclusion of reflective or contemplative exercises. They offer a way of averting the danger of inert ideas and enact Whitehead's recommendation: "What you teach, teach thoroughly."[17] But exactly what might this entail?

Rilke urged Franz Kappus to "live the questions." I would like to suggest that we can broaden his injunction to "live the questions, experiences, concepts, and ideas" that are part of every educational situation, in the classroom or outside it. In the interest of coverage, we normally rush through everything we teach. The physics demonstrations we do, the poems we read, the paintings we show are all quickly presented together with the relevant observations, scholarly gloss, and critical analysis. Students record these in their notebooks and ask the occasional question as they have been taught to do, but seldom do they internalize what they have learned, much less use it as an occasion for real personal development. Given how many courses are taught—with little care or attention for this kind of self-reflection—this cannot be a surprise. Yet shouldn't this be the ultimate aim of the classroom experience? As Barbara McClintock begged her Harvard student audience, take time with your material, adopt a contemplative stance toward it. Read the poem slowly and repeatedly, observe and reflect on the plant before you. Select a single line from the poem to hold in the mind until it begins to reveal its full multilayered significations. Live your way into each plant organ until you attain "a feeling for the organism."

Joel Upton at Amherst College and Joanna Ziegler at Holy Cross College are art historians who have developed pedagogies that take Whitehead and McClintock seriously.[18] They have independently crafted a staged contemplative engagement with one or two works of art over a full semester, with the conscious intent that students learn to "behold" a work of art on many levels. This requires time, repetition, patience, and practice. Stage by stage, students are led ever more deeply into the experiential learnings awaiting their

Experience, Contemplation, and Transformation

faithful attention. To begin with, students are bewildered, so different are such classes from their usual experience, but they quickly come to appreciate what is happening to them. They are learning at a level and depth that they did not know existed. Most become advocates for the transformative learning they experience at the hand of such contemplative and imaginative engagement, inquiry, and insight.[19]

In her final paper, Amherst student Caity Saggese offers her reflections on the impact of a course, Eros and Insight, that specifically incorporated contemplative and transformative elements:

> Before Amherst, life was like being stuck on a never ending merry-go-round with no way to stop it or even slow it down, and certainly no way to get off. I was on a whirlwind course, for sure, with no time to even consider other possibilities, other ways of living. Between schoolwork, the school newspaper, sports, volunteer work and club soccer, I barely had time to shower. So for me, Eros and Insight has been revolutionary, a real awakening that has prepared me not only for my next seven semesters here at Amherst College, but also for the rest of my life.
>
> Eros and Insight has awakened me to a new sense of possibilities and self-awareness. I feel as though I have already transformed in ways I did not know were possible. I now view the world around me in a new light: now I am aware that I am a part of the world, not merely an observer or one mechanically "passing through," and I know that I must participate in it . . . .
>
> So what does it all mean for me? It means that contemplation is key. If "every object well contemplated creates an organ for its perception," then I know that I must "create an organ" to understand myself first of all. I must figure out who I am and what I want. If Rilke recommended that we "stand guard over the solitude of the other," then I must first guard my own solitude to try to reach self-knowledge. In this sense, the very first part of my education will be self-discovery. That is, no more mindless merry-go-round. Instead, I must face

the fact that it is time to grow up and be mindful—deliberate. I tell myself I want to make a difference in the world, but in order to be able to do that I must learn, first about myself, and then about the world. So "organ formation" about the world is next, and is the path to a contemplative way of knowing/loving. This is the goal, for as Merton concluded, "it is the fullness of love that rejects nothing and no one, is open to ALL in ALL."

Many hundreds of professors around the country are now using such contemplative methods in their classes, sharing their experiences and pedagogical strategies at conferences and summer workshops each year.[20] In Appendix A, Mirabai Bush of the Center for Contemplative Mind in Society offers examples of how contemplative exercises have entered the classroom. In these and many similar classes, contemplative pedagogy has shown itself to be a powerful means of living the questions, experiences, concepts, and ideas of every class. Experiential and transformative learning is enhanced significantly thereby.

Contemplative pedagogy has found a home in every kind of institution of higher learning. Bradford Grant now teaches and acts as dean at Howard University using contemplative methods; David Haskell teaches at a college affiliated with the Episcopal Church; and Marilyn Nelson has taught her poetry and contemplation course at both a military academy and a secular state university. In faith-based colleges and universities an explicit emphasis is often given to reflection, calling, vocation, and life purpose, which offers a special opportunity for a contemplative curriculum. At the same time it raises the "messy" question of the place of religion and spirituality in higher education.

MEANING, PURPOSE, AND VALUES: SPIRITUALITY IN HIGHER EDUCATION

The relationship between spirituality and higher education is drawing increased attention in conferences, research, and publications.[21] Over the last several years UCLA's Higher Education Research

Institute (HERI) (a premier research and policy organization concerned with postsecondary education in the United States) has conducted surveys of over 100,000 students and 40,000 faculty in over 400 colleges and universities specifically about the intersection between spirituality and higher education. In its research studies, HERI asks,

> What role does spirituality play in the lives of today's college students? What is the connection between spirituality and religion? How do students' spiritual and religious qualities change during the college years, and how do such qualities relate to the students' academic and career development? How many students are actively engaged in a spiritual quest? What are colleges and universities doing that either encourages or inhibits students in this quest?[22]

The HERI research project was initiated in the belief that while there is justifiable pride in the outer accomplishments of higher education, the inner dimensions of education have been neglected: "Institutions have increasingly come to neglect the student's 'inner' development—the sphere of values and beliefs, emotional maturity, self-understanding, and spirituality."[23] For the purposes of the study, spirituality was defined as "how students make meaning of their education and their lives, how they develop a sense of purpose, and the value and belief dilemmas that they experience."

The five-year study was led by Alexander and Helen Astin and yielded a variety of important findings. First, interest in spirituality among students was found to be very widespread. The Astins' 2005 report indicated that 80 percent of 112,232 entering freshmen in 236 colleges and universities were interested in spirituality, with 41.8 percent of them reporting that "integrating spirituality into my life" was "essential" or "very important." Interestingly, this latter percentage increased to 50.4 percent for these students by the time they were juniors. Also while frequent religious observance declined significantly over the three years of the Astins' longitudinal study (from 43.7 percent to 25.4 percent), other measures of spirituality and ethical concern increased between freshman and junior years. The Astins also reported that college students have "high expectations for the role their institutions will play in their emotional and spiritual development." Specifically, the report finds that

> more than two-thirds (69%) consider it "essential" or "very important" that their college enhance their self-understanding and a similar proportion (67%) rate highly the role they want their college to play in developing their personal values. Nearly half (48%) also say it is "essential" or "very important" that colleges encourage their personal expression of spirituality.[24]

Even in a time of increased emphasis on the pragmatics of education for employment, we see that students still wish to explore the values, meaning, and purpose of their lives while in college. Parallel with the study of their major and the mastery of marketable skills, students long for a forum that can address their inner or spiritual concerns thoughtfully and deeply. If we are to educate the whole human being, then these dimensions of their nature cannot be forgotten. In fact, as Kronman has argued, our ways of teaching and learning should engage meaning, purpose, and values as an essential part of a college education for all young people.

With this in mind, I would like to point to the work of Larry Braskamp, Lois Trautvetter, and Kelly Ward, who have undertaken a three-year research project aimed at assessing how well ten faith-based colleges are doing in helping students to explore their identity, find their calling, and address the question of the "good life."[25] The emphasis Braskamp and his colleagues place on the conjoining of inner life with outer life and their view of being and doing as mutually reinforcing is resonant with the integrative philosophy of education we have been articulating. They, like us, seek a philosophy and practice of education that addresses the whole student. And the questions they pose can help to initiate transformative conversations across all parts of the campus, an outcome we applaud. (For a full description of this project, see Appendix A.)

SPIRITUALITY, EXPERIENCE, AND THE PROFESSORIATE

UCLA's Higher Education Research Institute (HERI) has performed similar research studies of the professoriate.[26] The findings of these studies are decidedly more mixed than those of the students. Professors agree with students concerning the high importance of values, meaning, and purpose in life, and they report that they personally cultivate them, but the role these should play in their teaching is unclear. Thus while student interest and expectations around spirituality are high, the academy is unsure of how to respond. But as Parker Palmer has remarked, this is one of the "messy" areas that cannot be avoided in a comprehensive treatment of higher education.

I have argued elsewhere that part of the conflict arises because we have an incorrect conceptual map of the academy and the place of spirituality within it.[27] The map places science and religion in opposition to one another. Where to locate contemplative spirituality is unclear. Negotiating the border between the domains of religion and science is a complicated and contentious matter. Our commitment to experience offers us an advantage when we come to the thorny question of the role of the religious and spiritual in higher education. To see why, we need to examine the role that experience and reason play in religion and in spirituality.

Following the neoorthodox position of Karl Barth and the non-overlapping magisteria (NOMA) of Stephen Jay Gould,[28] the pursuit of truth and knowledge has been seen as distinct and radically separate from the concerns of the faith traditions. They hold that universities, as institutions committed to knowledge and unfettered inquiry, should not concern themselves with matters of religion. In a very specific sense, I both agree and disagree with them. I agree that the practice of one's faith is a personal and private matter, especially on the campus of a secular university. Like the Astins, I distinguish, however, between religion and spirituality.

In my Amherst College course on science, values, and the spiritual traditions, we first engage the science-religion debate between such figures as the vocal atheist biologist Richard Dawkins and Francis Collins, who is head of the human genome project and an evangelical Christian. After a few weeks of reading authors on both sides of the science-religion debate, some students are tempted to agree with Gould that perhaps the best science and religion can achieve is a truce and a division of the territory. But then we consider the relation between science and what I term "cognitively oriented spirituality," and the tone and tenor of the encounter change dramatically. We read Goethe, William James, Rudolf Steiner, the Dalai Lama, Alan Wallace, and Ken Wilber (among others)—all of whom suggest some form of radical empiricism and the cultivation of contemplative or spiritual experience as a way to move beyond the divide. Here, the longing of students, as well as many faculty and staff, for academic engagement with the questions of meaning, values, and purpose finds a sound basis for fruitful conversations and common work. Spirituality can find its rightful place in our institutions if it accepts the challenge of knowledge. To do so means it must come to grips with the proper role of knowledge, experience, and reason in the domain of spirituality.

Harvard's motto, *Veritas*, or Truth, sums up the orientation embraced by most universities. The sanctioned methods for attaining the True are experience and reason, not revelation. The key question is how open or radical is one's stance toward experience. The Harvard philosopher and psychologist William James declared about his own radical empiricism, "To be radical, an empiricist must neither admit into its constructions any element that is not directly experienced nor exclude from them any element that is directly experienced."[29] James included in his empiricism all aspects of human experience and sought relentlessly for authentic religious and spiritual experience because he viewed such experience as important and open to development and investigation. Not surprisingly, in *Varieties of Religious Experience*, James emphasized the distinction between systematic dogmatic theology of church authorities and the firsthand experience of spiritual and religious life. To James's "radical empiricism" only the experience of the spiritual practitioner was germane to his budding "science of religions," for

Experience, Contemplation, and Transformation

he saw that the scriptural assertions of religion were not open to rebuttal by reasoned argumentation or empirical evidence.

Spiritual or contemplative experience, on the other hand, is open to all who practice contemplation and is, therefore, open also to thoughtful study. While not grounded in corporeal reality, to a radical empiricism or an ontology of experience the source of experience is of less concern than its clarity and quality. If inner, spiritual experience can be rigorously developed, carefully studied, and itself used as a mental instrument for investigation, then the consequences could be of revolutionary significance. As James wrote in *Pluralistic Universe*, "Let empiricism once become associated with religion, as hitherto, through some strange misunderstanding, it has been associated with irreligion, and I believe that a new era of religion as well as of philosophy will be ready to begin."[30]

Of special interest, therefore, are the traditions that have viewed spiritual knowledge as both possible and as an essential part of the path of liberation. One need only think of Gnosticism and Buddhism as examples. *Gnosis* means wisdom, and *prajna* is the practice of wisdom that releases one from suffering in classical Buddhist philosophy. Ignorance is the great cause of suffering in such systems. Whatever will dispel ignorance has the power also to mitigate suffering. The Burmese Nobel Peace Prize laureate Aung San Suu Kyi was once asked if she believed in evil. She replied, "I don't think that there is such a thing as evil, but I think there is such a thing as ignorance and the root of all evil is ignorance."

For this reason, in his meetings with scientists the Dalai Lama is at pains to indicate his rejection of dogma and his openness to the clearly reasoned arguments of science and the power of experimental evidence, even if these run contrary to the teachings of the Buddha. In fact, the Buddha himself recommended such openness. Buddhist philosophy offers its own reasoned arguments and inner experience as evidence for its views. Should scientific evidence prevail, then the theological positions of Buddhism can be changed. In this way the Dalai Lama agrees with Whitehead's assessment, "Religion will not regain its old power until it can face change in the same spirit as does science."[31] Truth has the power to liberate, but ignorance binds us to delusions and so to suffering. The Dalai Lama, however, also is clear that the materialist metaphysics that is often assumed by scientists is not really a legitimate part of science itself, which is agnostic concerning metaphysical questions.

In light of these considerations, I have come to distinguish cognitively oriented spirituality from faith-based religious life. In the former, empirical knowledge and imaginative insight have a place. In the latter, revelation was only given to the original authors of scripture, and later theologians are restricted to interpreting the texts left behind. In this way, the map that divides the two magisteria of science and religion is wrong. Spirituality can become a practice that leads to knowledge based in experience. As such it finds a home on the side of science. But it is equally concerned with values, meaning, and purpose, and so it shares much in common with religion. Cognitively oriented spirituality, therefore, confounds the simplistic dichotomy of science and religion, or knowledge versus faith. It redefines the entire discussion. James was correct in his view that the association of empiricism with religion would be revolutionary.

Not all denominations reject contemporary spiritual experience. Indeed, most faith traditions have a mystical or charismatic wing that embraces continued spiritual practice and experience, and so turns toward experiential and even cognitively oriented spirituality. In my work with faith-based colleges and universities, I have experienced a special openness, even an eagerness to engage the moral and spiritual life of students. The possibilities of moving the discussion beyond scriptural exegesis or dogmatics and toward experience is attractive to many at those institutions. Quaker silence, *meditatio,* and *contemplatio* place the practitioner in a state of receptivity that invites primary religious experience and understanding.

The place of James's revolution in the relation between religion and science can and should be in the halls and classrooms of academe.

We possess, at least in principle, the freedom, wit, and collegiality to invite all who are interested—students, faculty, and staff—into this long-delayed but highly significant conversation.

BEYOND THE PAST

Surveying the previous chapters will, I hope, convince the reader that we are not advocating a return to some golden era in higher education. Even as we acknowledge the losses that have occurred in recent decades, we also recognize the great strides that have been made in access to higher education, in the sophistication of instruction within the disciplines, and in their application to real-world problems. We see none of this as incommensurate with the exploration of questions of purpose, meaning, and values. The undergraduate years remain an ideal time to engage with the largest issues in life.

In *Education's End*, Anthony Kronman advocates for the disciplined exploration of life's purpose and value through the careful study of great literature and philosophy.[32] He observes that in the period from the Harvard presidency of Charles Eliot (1869–1909) until the 1960s, the humanities were the locus wherein such questions were raised, and Kronman argues persuasively for a return to that practice as exemplified by Yale's Directed Studies program. But does the study of the humanities offer the only occasion for the disciplined study of life's purpose? I hope that it is clear from the discussion and examples in these chapters that there are numerous venues for such explorations, whether it is helping Mayan children in the Yucatán to read or in an economics class that truly engages, perhaps with the help of contemplative exercises, the real suffering caused by the inequities of our economic system.

The philosophy of education we have advanced here is not a return to the past but is directed toward the future. By expanding our ontology to embrace the interconnectedness of reality and its multiple dimensions, by extending our epistemology to include contemplative, aesthetic, and moral knowing, by recognizing the

122

ethical dimensions of our way of knowing, we can grow the exploration of purpose beyond the humanities to all aspects of curricular and co-curricular life. Integrative education can and should happen across the campus and beyond it and bring with it a deep and pervasive engagement with the questions of meaning and purpose.

Chapter 6

Transformative Conversations on Campus[*]

Parker J. Palmer

A CONVERSATIONAL STRATEGY OF CHANGE

We began by exploring the nature of integrative education—the kind of education that, as we said in the Introduction, can address "the hungers and needs of our students, the abiding questions of the human adventure, and the social, economic,

---

[*] The concept of "transformative conversations" that I explore in this chapter is central to the work of the Center for Courage & Renewal. See http://www.couragerenewal.org. A brief summary of the ideas behind the Center's work can be found in a document titled "Foundations of the Circle of Trust® Approach," available at http://www.couragerenewal.org/about/foundations. For a detailed exploration of those ideas, see Parker J. Palmer, *A Hidden Wholeness: The Journey Toward an Undivided Life* (San Francisco: Jossey-Bass, 2004).

and political challenges of our time." We then looked at some of the basic philosophical and pedagogical issues raised by this approach to teaching and learning. Next we took a more detailed look—especially through the lens of the "new sciences"—at some key features of integrative education's philosophical underpinnings.

In this chapter, we turn to "putting wheels" on the idea of transforming the academy through collegial conversations. How might we collaborate with others on our campuses to pursue issues in the philosophy of education, their implications and implementation, in ways that could move higher education closer to the integrative ideal? What kind of on-campus vehicles might be used by faculty, administrators, students, alumni, and others to continue the conversation about integrative education, face-to-face, in real time, with real results?

Anyone who cares about social change can quote Margaret Mead's well-known comment from memory: "Never doubt that a small group of thoughtful, committed citizens can change the world. Indeed, it is the only thing that ever has." The second half of that statement is clearly not true (some social change comes from the very centers of power that citizens must organize to resist), but the first half is self-evident—if that small group of people has the skill and the will to translate thoughtfulness and commitment into socially transformative action. From a handful of citizens insisting that the school board pay attention to students with special needs, to hundreds of thousands joining hands to end the evils of slavery or apartheid, much of the emending of history has been sparked by small circles of people talking and listening to each other respectfully, reflectively, and intentionally.

In the mid 1970s, I sat in a circle of rocking chairs at the Highlander Research and Education Center in Tennessee.[1] Twenty years earlier, when it was known as the Highlander Folk School, this organization had hosted a series of conversations between blacks and whites that planted the seeds of the American civil rights movement. Having sat in that circle with knowledge of what flowed from it, I find it impossible to forget a simple fact: significant social change can come from people who share a concern sitting, rocking, and talking with each other—if they are willing to speak honestly and act competently on what they learn about themselves and each other. Among the participants in that original Highlander circle were Rosa Parks, Martin Luther King, Jr., and many others whose names are not so well-known. As they rocked and talked, exploring personal stories, institutional conditions and the theory and tactics of nonviolent social change, they generated change of historic proportions.

Like most institutions, the academy is notoriously resistant to change, so resistant that academics like to lampoon themselves: "Changing a university is like trying to move a cemetery. You get no help from the inhabitants." Part of the problem is that few universities I know have anything like a circle of Tennessee rocking chairs, hospitable spaces where "the inhabitants" can sit and talk in an open, honest, and intentional way about their concerns as educators. If such conversations can help spark a civil rights movement, why could they not help spark educational reform? The university may be slow to change, but surely it is not as intransigent as American racism.

In Chapter 3, Arthur Zajonc referred to the "divisions that fragment us and our world." Those divisions, rooted in our failure to recognize the reality of interconnectedness, are found not only in the ontology, epistemology, pedagogy, and ethics that form a silent backdrop to university life. They are reflected in the fragmentation of our personal relationships within the academy. Ask a sample of faculty if they have found "the community of scholars" they thought they were joining when they started down this trail, and more than a few will respond with a sigh, a rueful smile, or rolled eyes. When professors are able to name a meaningful experience of "the community of scholars," it is more likely to be among members of their far-flung disciplinary guilds than with colleagues on their campus.

For the past thirty years, I have spoken with faculty across the country about the "privatization of the professoriate" and the "pain of disconnection"—from colleagues, from students, and from their own original passions—underlying conditions of academic life that faculty do not talk much about, but whose symptoms are common among them. I cannot remember a single time when a professor said to me, "You are wrong about all that." Fragmentation of this sort is, of course, encouraged by the very structures of the academy. Not only are faculty isolated in silos called disciplines and departments, but the conception of "one's work" in academia is itself privatized: we close the doors of our offices to do our research and close the doors of our classrooms to do our teaching, out of view of colleagues in both cases.

A classic method of maintaining institutional status quo is to create a system that isolates people from one another, keeping the sparks of change from jumping from one person to the next and preventing a critical mass of change agents from forming. In every case of that sort I can think of, the separation imposed upon people soon gets reinforced by personal choice: people who live under structural isolation eventually internalize the desire for isolation because of the negative stereotypes and mutual fears that come from not knowing one another. That is the kind of isolation that the Highlander conversations were designed to break down, because isolation helped maintain racism's stranglehold on American culture.

CONVERSATION AS ANTIDOTE AND TACTIC

In this chapter, I take a cue from the Highlander experience and explore that "meeting of the minds" we call conversation as both an antidote to academic isolation and a tactic for institutional change. My thesis is simple: the conversation of colleagues is a critical element in advancing the cause of integrative education. My recommendation is equally simple: if advancing integrative education is your goal, find people you can talk with about your concerns and visions of possibility. Sit with at least one or two other stakeholders and explore approaches to education that honor diverse ways of knowing, teaching, and learning, approaches that can help students learn how to hold intellectual complexity and prepare them to play multiple and responsible roles in the ecosystem of adult life.

Much of this chapter is aimed at encouraging conversation between faculty colleagues. But the word *stakeholders* is an important reminder that creative change in higher education has, can, and must come in partnership with people other than faculty. Some of these partners are, of course, administrators who support integrative education. (In Appendix C, you will find three stories that show the power of academic leaders to help set integrative processes in motion—and the power of conversation to create the conditions for change. Thomas Coburn, president of Naropa University, engaged the full college community in creating a faculty "Council of Elders" to help him better understand the concerns of the community and build trust between administration and faculty, the kind of trust that can spill over into the challenges of transforming curriculum and pedagogy. President Beverly Tatum and faculty members at Spelman College created President and Faculty Dinners to make a space for open and honest exchange among the faculty and the president, another way of creating spillovers of life-giving energy. Dennis Huffman, program supervisor at Prince George's Community College, found ways to generate meaningful conversation between his part-time and widely dispersed faculty, many of whom spend little time on campus.)

And why do we so often forget the key stakeholders called alumni and alumnae when it comes to educational reform? They can become significant partners in transformative conversations on campus, as the case of Princeton University's Project 55 reveals.[2] In 1989, alumni from the class of 1955 came together to consider a thirty-fifth reunion gift to their alma mater. Members of this class had spent several decades doing significant work in the world beyond Princeton's walls; their gratitude for their Princeton education was accompanied by an awareness of how much they had had to unlearn to engage the world's problems deeply and well.

So, rather than donate a memorial garden or a bell tower, they rented office space adjacent to the campus and hired a small staff to help their alma mater integrate its curriculum more thoroughly with the needs of the world. With administrative approval, these alumni funded and mounted Project 55's flagship effort, the Princeton Public

Interest Program, which in just a few years created so many service-learning internships and fellowships that it became the largest single source of employment for enrolled Princeton students.

In 1996, Project 55 gathered Princeton alumni from the 1950s through the 1990s around a white paper titled "Princeton University in the 21st Century: Paths to More Effective Undergraduate Education (A Proposal from Affectionate Alumnae and Alumni)."[3] "We are proud of our university," the paper begins, and "we want to make a case for a new approach to undergraduate education at Princeton that takes account of research that ... suggests new curricular and pedagogical approaches" that are responsive to how students learn and to the needs of the world. Today, the influence of Project 55 has gone deeper and wider than its founders could possibly have envisioned.

The moral of this story is simple: as you look around for conversation partners, make sure you are not wearing blinders: think unconventionally. Who has more reason to care about the kind of education an institution offers than alumni who have benefited from the best of it and suffered from the worst of it? So why are alumni so rarely regarded as partners in educational reform? Surely, alumni involvement and resources accelerated the pace of this particular change at Princeton well beyond what faculty and administrators could have done by themselves.

A parallel case can be made for student involvement in transformative conversations. We do not have a self-contained case study to prove the point, but we do have the evidence provided by a critical movement that has changed the face of higher education over the past forty years: without student initiative, service learning might never have taken root across the country. And without student buy-in, service learning would certainly not have spread as far and wide as it has.

A conversational strategy of change requires initiative in taking an action that is against the current of much of academic life: reaching out to each other and actually getting together. In a culture of privatization and overload, this will not be an easy sell. But despite these obstacles, on every campus I have ever visited there is a core

THE HEART OF HIGHER EDUCATION

group of visionaries who yearn for something better and have the capacity to reach out to the next concentric circle of people, inviting them into a conversation that holds the promise of planting seeds of change. How to hold those conversations in a way that maximizes this promise is the focus of the rest of this chapter.

Toward Transformative Conversations

Not every conversation is transformative. In fact, few are, and there is a reason for that. Many encounters that might become transformative are used to put the spotlight on ourselves or persuade others of the rightness of our facts and theories, values and beliefs. We are driven not so much by egomania as by ingrained habits of discourse that make talking with each other far less than it could be, sometimes creating outcomes that drive us apart instead of bringing us together.

Here is a simple example of what I mean. You and I are talking, and you mention a work-related problem you are trying to solve or an issue you are wrestling with. I listen until you finish, and then I either tell you what I would do about your problem or, more likely, tell a parallel story of my own. *Parallel* is exactly the right word for conversations where two people never intersect to illumine and inspire one another but merely run alongside each other for a while until they veer off into isolation again, usually leaving both of them feeling unheard.

We can change that dance, and in a moment I will explore some practical ways to do it. But first I need to address three attitudes that sometimes keep academics who want to see institutional change from doing anything about it: "I am a teacher and scholar, not a reformer"; "Even if I wanted to be a reformer, professors are powerless to create change"; and "I am alone on my campus in my educational values and visions."

Is "reformer" the job of a teacher and a scholar? The answer depends on whether your vision for higher education requires institutional change that allows you to live into that vision. Some faculty feel at home within the current academic division of labor while others feel like strangers in a strange land. But until we have more opportunities for "transformative conversations," few will have a chance to explore and perhaps expand their educational vision or find colleagues who might join them in a shared effort to pursue that vision.

The notion that professors are powerless to effect change is ironic at best and a poor excuse for inaction at worst. Powerless in comparison to whom? Faculty have more power than most working people and, once tenured, more security to use their power—certainly more than the folks who gathered in that circle of rocking chairs at the Highlander Folk School. And if a conversational approach to planting the seeds of change has any merit whatsoever, then faculty have special competencies for this version of change agency.

Good scholars understand inquiry as a way of being in the world, and the skills that are key to inquiry are also key to transformative conversations. Good scholars, for example, know how to ask honest, open questions of the phenomena they study—the artifacts of history, sociological statistics, the way a novelist uses language, the data that emerge from a particle accelerator. No scholar worth his or her salt conducts a "parallel conversation" with the phenomena, changing the subject when the phenomena speak rather than listening deeply to what they are trying to say.

Good scholars keep asking honest, open questions of the phenomena they are studying, questions meant to deepen understanding of what that reality is all about. They reach conclusions and think about implications only when the inquiry feels complete, all the while expecting a next round of questions, conclusions and implications. The problem is not that we do not know how to do this kind of thing. The problem is that we do so little of it with each other. If we would do nothing more than come together with a few colleagues and ask *them* the kinds of questions that we ask of the phenomena we study—questions about *their* experiences and visions as educators—and then seek points of theoretical and applied convergence between us, we would take a first step toward becoming agents of change.

That is exactly what happened at Highlander in the midfifties. The people in that circle sat looking at each other across a racial divide at least as baffling as the divide between the human mind and the world of subatomic physics or preliterate *Homo sapiens*, a divide far more perilous than the divides between academic disciplines. They began to close that divide as they conducted an honest, open inquiry into each other's experience: "What is it like to be black in mid-twentieth-century America?" "What it is like to be white in this place and time?" As they asked, they listened. As they listened, they understood. And as they understood, they came together in a next round of inquiry about goals and the actions required to move toward those goals together.

Those of us who understand inquiry, for whom it is a way of being in the world, can use our understanding to reach across gaps, ask each other questions that matter, listen with care, and find our way toward personal and communal action. In small groups like the one at Highlander, we can give each other a chance to recall the commitments and passions that brought us into academic life. We can ask how supported we feel in those commitments today and share our hopes for a more supportive academic environment, perhaps finding common cause. We can move beyond grousing to generating a community of dialogue and the empowerment that comes with it.

Which brings me to the third attitudinal obstacle I have found among faculty: the conviction that one's values and visions are not shared by colleagues, so there is no one with whom to join in community. Years ago, as my travel schedule frequently took me to campuses to give lectures and lead workshops, I noticed how often someone would say to me privately, "I believe in the kind of change you're advocating, but I'm the only person on this campus who feels that way." And by the time I had finished a two- or three-day visit to a campus, six or eight people had told me exactly the same thing.

So instead of commiserating with them, I began asking, "What have you done to test your notion that you are all alone with your values and visions? I understand that the dominant culture here offers you little support. But what have you done to send off signals that might allow kindred spirits to spot you so that you could reach out to each other?" Almost always, the answer was, "Nothing."

I empathize with these people. I have been where they are, wanting to see something change but unable or unwilling to take even small steps in that direction, or simply not knowing how. But the time comes when one needs to take that first step and give up the self-fulfilling conviction of isolation that has helped to create a culture of "veto power" in the academy—a culture where saying no to proposals for change too easily becomes the norm, or where the absence of community and encouragement make it unlikely that visions for change will arise in the first place.

There is another source of stasis in the academy, sometimes called "paralysis by analysis." The habits of thinking big and thinking critically can serve us well in the world of ideas but may fail us in the world of action, where they can quickly lead to a sense of being overwhelmed by impossible goals. The conversational strategy begins as an exercise in thinking small to take things to a human scale; the telling of small personal stories at the Highlander Folk School helped plant the seeds of a large and complex movement that made American history. Of course, there is no guarantee that starting a small conversation will lead to something larger. But the failure to take any step at all, no matter how small, comes with an ironclad guarantee that we will not be part of helping change happen.

The step required to plant the seeds of change can be as small as one of us reaching out to one other. My conversation partner and co-author Arthur Zajonc did exactly that, with remarkable results. Here he describes the beginning of an important collaboration:

> Nearly twenty years ago I applied to a foundation and received
> support for a series of campuswide talks by distinguished
> visitors that included Saul Bellow, the astronaut Rusty
> Schweickart, and the cultural historian William Irwin
> Thompson. The series was entitled Re-imagining the Human
> in a Technological Age. I felt then, as now, that the image we
> have of the human being was not rich and deep enough to meet
> the demands of our technological age.

The Heart of Higher Education

One faculty member came to all of the talks, someone I did not know. At the final talk I approached him, introduced myself, and asked who he was. His name was Joel Upton, an art historian at Amherst, who said that he had found all of the talks compelling, and each even more so than the one before. In that moment, we began a friendship and series of collaborations that continue to this day.

Our first joint venture was to launch an interdisciplinary class called by the same name: Re-imagining the Human in a Technological Age. Since then, Upton and I have continued with other collaborations. Our current one is the First-Year Seminar Eros and Insight that explores the relationship between love and what we term contemplative knowing.

I have come to see my initial "Re-imagining" lecture series as a way for me, a physicist, to show the range of my interests and questions. It was a way of "running up a flag" to see if anyone else was open to and interested in the things I most cared about.

I will return to the Upton-Zajonc collaboration later in this chapter because it demonstrates the power of a transformative conversation to spread ripples far beyond the first stone dropped into the pond. For the moment, I want simply to point out that when people talk meaningfully with each other, the unpredictable can happen, unpredictable even to the person who is about to be transformed.

Myles Horton, the founder of the Highlander Folk School, makes this point wonderfully well with a little-known story about the time he introduced Rosa Parks, a participant in the Highlander conversations, to Eleanor Roosevelt:

Mrs. Roosevelt asked . . . "Have you been called a Communist yet, Mrs. Parks?" When Rosa answered yes, Mrs. Roosevelt said, "I suppose Myles told you when you were at Highlander that you'd be called a Communist." Rosa told her I hadn't warned her, and Mrs. Roosevelt criticized me for [that]. I said, "If I'd known what she was going to do, I'd have told her. But when she was at Highlander, she said she wasn't going to do

135

anything. She said that ... the white people wouldn't let the black people do anything, and besides, the black people hadn't been willing to stick together, so she didn't think she'd do anything. I didn't see any reason to tell a person who wasn't going to do anything that she'd be branded as a Communist.... If I'd known she was going to start the civil rights movement, I'd have told her." And Rosa said, "Yes, he told me later on, after I got arrested."[4]

As Rosa Parks sat in that circle at Highlander, she was being prepared inwardly *and* unknowingly to make a crucial decision, the decision to live "divided no more." On December 1, 1955, in Montgomery, Alabama, when she refused to yield her seat on the bus to a white man with "superior rights," she was saying, with her action, "I will no longer behave on the outside in a way that contradicts a truth I hold deeply on the inside, the truth that we are born equal and entitled to equal treatment under the laws of both man and God."

The decision to live an undivided life—made by people who know what they truly value—has always been a sparking point of social change. Higher education can grow into its fullest potentials if more and more academics will make "the Rosa Parks decision." The historical record of what happened soon after Rose Parks sat in that circle of rocking chairs and made her public witness offers hope, rooted in reality, that under the right conditions—conditions we can help shape—a conversation that moves one or two people can move many more, move them to action that transforms institutional cultures. Later in this chapter, I will explore that possibility in more detail. But first, I want to look more closely at what makes a conversation transformative.

Hosting a Transformative Conversation

The outcomes of talking with one another depend as much on whom we talk with, where we talk with them, and how we talk to one another as they do on what we talk about. We have focused heavily in this book on the *what* question. Here I want to say a few words about questions of *who* and *where* before turning to the all-important *how* question in some detail.

As you ask yourself who might share your interest in integrative education, cast the net wide: consider faculty, administrators, students, staff, alumni, and anyone else who is a stakeholder in the nature of education on your campus. Your accuracy in "reading" people is important as you take this first step. It is distressing to start a small and vulnerable conversation with a handful of people, only to find that one of them has a spirit so toxic that the seeds of insight die before they can germinate.

In the first few rounds of such conversations, the point is not to convert the resistant but to cultivate the possible by collaborating with people who hope to bring it into being. Once the group develops a culture strong enough to support generative dialogue around significant ideas, some skeptics can and often should be brought in—partly to test the ideas against their resistance, partly to offer them something that they might find worthy of their best energies.

But even with the best possible first-round people, the capacity of any conversation to take us to the deeper reaches of our lives—to tap into those values, visions, and energies that might lead us to become agents of change—depends on whether we experience the space between us as safe for taking relational risks and reaching for what Lincoln called "the better angels of our nature." Unfortunately, in professional life at large, we seem most adept at creating spaces that invite our "lesser angels" to show up.

In academic life, these are the angels that want to blame this or that on students, colleagues, or the administration; the ones that want to do little more than argue over parking spaces or credit hours; the ones that want to engage in intellectual one-upmanship; the ones that want nothing more than to win the argument. Once we have been in a few spaces of that sort, conversation loses its luster, feeding the privatization of academic life that inhibits creative change.

Those of us who want to host conversations that are generative for ourselves and our institutions must be intentional about creating spaces that are hospitable to the human spirit as we make ourselves vulnerable to honest exchanges, new ideas, and hopes for change. I do not intend to offer an Emily Post handbook of conversational etiquette, as if you had no idea of what makes for a hospitable space. Good teachers create such spaces all the time, spaces that invite generative discourse in the classroom. The quickest way to find out what "hospitable space" means to you is to ask yourself a simple question: under what conditions do I feel enough trust and freedom to explore some of the "big questions and worthy dreams" that bear on my vocation?[5]

Here are some of my answers to that question, offered not as a how-to-do-it manual but as a brief tour of the challenges and the potentials of hosting a generative conversation. The first thing that comes to mind when I think about "feeling at home" enough to settle into genuine dialogue is physical ambience. Conference rooms with flickering fluorescent lights, hospital-green walls, and people sitting behind tables as if behind ramparts do not work for me, and colleges and universities have too many such spaces. What works is the "hominess" suggested by that circle of rocking chairs, which is why I invite people into my office or my living room for a cup of tea when I want to talk about something that has personal meaning and importance.

Next, I find that a conversation that begins with ideas is not as easy to relax into as one that begins with personal experiences, which is where the Highlander conversations began. "What do you *think* about X, Y, or Z?" quickly takes me into my intellect, where defensiveness may arise as I wonder whether I can articulate my thoughts and how my conversation partner will respond. But "Tell me a *story* about X, Y, or Z" feels safe because it is unlikely that anyone will tell me that my story is mistaken. And the invitation to tell a story immediately calls me toward an integrative way of thinking, since a story must be told in the round, with feelings as well as facts and concepts.

There is an even deeper reason why personal stories are more likely to weave the kinds of relationships forged in that circle of

THE HEART OF HIGHER EDUCATION

rocking chairs. It is not uncommon for people to work side by side for years without knowing much more about each other at retirement than they did on day one. As a result, many of us bear the wound of invisibility, believing, not without reason, that no matter how hard or how well we work, no one really sees us. When we invite each other to tell our stories, we have a chance to create community in the simple act of saying "I see you."

Storytelling can create community at an even deeper level: the more one knows about another person's story, the less one is able to dislike or distrust, let alone despise, that person. This is a good thing in and of itself, but it serves a larger purpose as well by helping us weave a more resourceful and resilient collegiality. At some point down the road, when we need to solve a problem or deal with a difficult conflict, we are more likely to have woven the fabric of relationships required to do it well.

To demonstrate this "secret hidden in plain sight," we can cite social science data as well as common sense. As I mentioned in Chapter 2, a study of Chicago's efforts at school reform during the 1990s showed that the most powerful driver of improved educational outcomes for kids is not money, curriculum, technique, or governance.[6] It is relational trust between teachers, teachers and administrators, and teachers and parents. So community and the trust-building it requires is not an optional exercise to be dismissed as touchy-feely—not if we care about deepening our institution's capacity to pursue its mission.

An invitation to talk about ourselves and our journeys can take us out of our emotional comfort zone, especially those of us who were taught to say and write "It is thought . . . " instead of "I think . . . ." So the host of a transformative conversation must lower the risk level by asking autobiographical questions that are not gratuitously intimate but are clearly related to the larger purpose of this conversation: to pursue a grounded, thoughtful, and practical inquiry into the philosophy and practice of integrative education. Here are some examples of the kind of storytelling prompts I have in mind, each of them intended to begin with personal experience but open toward the larger issues involved in "uncovering the heart of higher education":

- What took you into your academic career? What were some of the inner and outer drivers that moved you in this direction?

- To what extent have your original aspirations for an academic career been fulfilled or thwarted? What have been some of the work-related highs and lows?

- When you set out on your academic career, did you have a vision of higher education and your place in it? What were the sources of that vision? To what extent has that vision been fulfilled?

- Tell a story about a teacher who made a significant impact on you. What made him or her an important person in your development? What do you learn about your own learning style from recalling that teacher's impact?

- Tell a story that reveals some of the core needs of today's students as you perceive them. What are some of your long-term hopes for the kind of education you and we might offer them? What kinds of support or resources would help us move in that direction?

- Tell a story about something you've done to make your own teaching a more integrative enterprise, such as connecting your subject more closely to your students' lives, team teaching interdisciplinary courses, building a bridge between your subject and the larger community as in service learning, or collaborating with the student-life staff on learning-related projects.

- Tell a story about something you've done to take your own research in a more integrative direction, such as drawing on disciplines other than your own, collaborating with specialists in other fields, or connecting your research to real-time problem-solving.

- Tell a story about models of integrative education you've seen elsewhere, in teaching or research or both, that struck you as worthy of emulation.

Moving from Stories to Ideas

If the point of these conversations is to explore the philosophy of integrative education and ways of implementing it, why begin the process with personal storytelling instead of cutting to the chase? Because when we start from our own experience, moving from "the heart of an educator" to "the heart of higher education," the means are congruent with the end: we ground a discussion of integrative education in a place of personal integration, a place where our thinking is integrated with the hurts, hopes, and animating forces of our own vocational journeys. The integrative ideas and programs most likely to get traction are rooted in personal need, from which comes commitment, another truth behind the impact of the Highlander conversations. Service learning, for example, was sparked by students and faculty who knew that something important was lacking in higher education.

So as you begin to guide the conversation more deeply into ideas, try to stay connected with the personal stories that have been told, referring back to them and weaving them in and out of your exploration of theory and practice. Doing so can help people move toward "the Rosa Parks decision," the decision to live an undivided life, to witness our deepest educational values in ways that plant the seeds of transformation.

For the past five chapters, we have explored a wide range of foundational issues in integrative education. These materials—and, more importantly, the ideas that you and your conversation partners bring to the circle—offer ample grist for your conversational mill. So instead of presenting a list of discussion topics here, I want to focus on some of the methods of exploring the topics that emerge from the stories you have told each other that will give your conversation the best chance to bear fruit.[7]

The methods I advocate are nothing new, and they are certainly not "countercultural." They are rooted in principles of inquiry at the heart of the academic tradition, principles we tend to honor more in the breach than the observance as we relate to each other. If we are to change that dance, the host of a transformative conversations needs to be hospitable *and* firm, inviting an open conversation *and* establishing ground rules that help sustain the inquiry and move it toward next steps.

For example, in everyday chitchat (as I noted above), when we hear someone's story we tend to respond with a story of our own. But that kind of "parallel storytelling" can keep us from learning all that might be learned from the first story and leave the speaker feeling unheard. So the host of a transformative conversation must invite people to stay in "inquiry mode" for a while by asking the storyteller honest, open questions about what he or she has said. Such questions have the power, in the words of Nelle Morton, to "hear people into speech," deeper and deeper speech.[8] This not only helps people feel heard but helps them tell their story in greater depth, improving the odds that both the speaker and the listeners will learn something new.

What are the earmarks of an open, honest question? First and foremost, an honest, open question is one you cannot possibly ask while thinking to yourself, "I know the right answer to this and I sure hope you give it to me." For instance, "Have you ever thought about seeing a therapist?" is *not* an honest, open question! In contrast, these are honest and open questions: "What experience shaped the idea you just told us about?" "You said that your students are resistant to this approach. What are the marks of that resistance, and what do you think causes it?" "You mentioned you find the work of such-and-such a writer helpful. What is that work, and why it is meaningful to you?"

These questions come from genuine curiosity and authentic inquiry, just as good scholarship does. They do not put the speaker on the defensive. They do not attempt to compel the speaker to go in a particular direction. They allow the speaker to define his or her

THE HEART OF HIGHER EDUCATION

truth for himself or herself. Here are a few more guidelines to help you encourage the discipline of asking honest, open questions:

- Try not to get ahead of the language used by the person you are questioniing. "What did you mean when you said X?" is an honest, open question. "Didn't you mean to mention Y?" is not.

- Ask questions that are brief and to the point rather than larding them with rationales and background information that allow you to insert your own opinions or advice. But avoid questions with yes-no or right-wrong answers.

- Ask questions that go to the person as well as the problem, questions about the inner realities of the situation as well as the outward facts.

- Ask questions aimed at helping the speaker explore his or her story, concern, or issue rather than satisfying your own curiosity.

- If you have an intuition that a certain question might be useful, even if it seems a bit off-the-wall, trust it—once you are reasonably certain that it is an honest, open question.

- If you aren't sure about a particular question, sit with it for a while and wait for clarity.

- Watch the pacing of the questions. Questions that come too fast may feel aggressive, cutting off the deep reflection that can help focus the person.

- In a group of any size, if you have asked one question and heard an answer, you may feel a need to ask a follow-up question. But if you find yourself about to ask the third question in a row before anyone else has had a chance to ask one, don't.[9]

As the conversation proceeds under a good host's guidance, everyone in turn gets a chance to put his or her thoughts, feelings, and experiences into the circle and to elaborate on them under the

Transformative Conversations on Campus

honest, open questioning of other people. We do not criticize each other's ideas; we probe them for understanding. If my ideas differ from yours, I am free to express them when my turn comes. But I do so as a statement of my truth, not as a rebuttal of yours, and as I articulate my truth, I take care not to phrase it as a rebuttal. If you say "X" and later I say "not-X," it is condescending to begin my statement by saying, "I think you were wrong about that. Here's how I see it." Everyone understands that "not-X" is different from "X," so there is no need to underscore my difference with you. Prefacing what I have to say by rebutting someone else creates an adversarial atmosphere that chills out vulnerable speaking and leads to ego-driven tensions that rarely take us to worthwhile destinations.

At this point, you may be wondering how a conversation of this sort can take us anywhere at all. How do we drive toward a conclusion or a decision, let alone an action plan, if all we do is listen to each other and ask questions? How can we possibly separate the wheat from the chaff using this sort of "open inquiry" approach? Where is the critique of ideas and proposals that are the stuff of real decision making? And when do we "take the vote" to determine who is right and who is wrong, or at least who wins and who loses?

When a conversation of the sort I am proposing is well-done, the result is remarkable: people start correcting themselves, sorting out what makes sense from what does not, and the group proves to be smarter than the sum of its parts. When we all speak from our own center to the center of the circle and allow ourselves to reflect on what has been put out there, a new kind of thinking sets in. In the reflective calm of that kind of conversation, we may start to see that apparent opposites have something in common, that there are ways to bridge ideas that, held aggressively in debate, get driven further apart. (Such a conversation was held at Wellesley College as one president's tenure came to an end. The issues were difficult and discouraging, but the way the group process was held by its conveners allowed the conversation to have a generative and regenerative outcome. See the essay in Appendix C by Diana Chapman Walsh and Patricia Byrne.)

The phrase "in the reflective calm of that kind of conversation" deserves its own reflective moment. Throughout this chapter, I have been appealing to one of the ancient and abiding values of academic culture, the value of reflective inquiry. While some degree of reflection is still alive in labs, libraries (bricks-and-mortar and online), and advanced seminars, the academy has largely lost one of its most critical preconditions: the quietude that allows for real reflection on what we have seen and heard, felt, and thought, a quietude that has been overwhelmed by overactivity and frenzy of the same sort found in many workplaces.

Again, one of the academy's taproots is the monastery, a bastion of quietude established in the fourth century where young men could receive the only sort of formal schooling available at the time. But as the scope of schooling expanded, the quietude declined and disappeared. Our lives are so frenetic, and our models of inquiry so argumentative, aggressive, and even combative, that we do not even know what we have lost. But a brief excursion into etymology will remind us:

> *School*: "place of instruction," O.E. *scol*, from L. *schola*, from Gk. *skhole* "school, lecture, discussion," also "leisure, spare time," originally "a holding back, a keeping clear" .... The original notion is "leisure," which passed to "otiose discussion," then "place for such."[10]

It is almost inconceivable that the university as a whole will ever reclaim those qualities of leisure, of holding back and keeping clear, of becoming a place for "otiose discussion," discussion that has no practical goal. But those are among the conditions under which creativity flourishes, and those conditions can be reclaimed in small groups gathered within the university and proceeding by ground rules such as those I propose here.

Abraham Flexner, one of the great twentieth-century reformers of higher and professional education, wrote words we would do well to remember: "Quite clearly ... the same conditions that

Transformative Conversations on Campus

permit idleness, neglect, or perfunctory performance of duty are necessary to the highest exertions of human intelligence."[11]

From Stories and Ideas to Action

How can a conversation between two or three people go beyond *exploring* integrative education toward experimenting with and implementing some form of it? The story of Arthur Zajonc and Joel Upton offers one obvious answer, as these two professors, one of physics, the other of fine arts, were drawn by their conversations to create first one and then another team-taught course. Their active response to the ideas that arose between them has drawn significant administrative support and considerable attention on their campus, as noted in a feature article in the Spring 2004 issue of *Amherst Magazine*, focused on their first-year seminar, Eros and Insight.[12]

The story of the Zajonc-Upton collaboration does not end there, however; it provides evidence that the outcomes of a transformative conversation between colleagues can travel beyond one campus. Arthur Zajonc has lectured on this collaboration at Brown University, the University of Michigan, Georgetown University, The University of Massachusetts at Amherst, Dartmouth College, Bryn Mawr College, and Haverford College, as well as at universities in Edinburgh, Paris, and Munich. It has been written about in *The Journal of Cognitive Affective Learning*, *The Journal of College and Character*, *Teachers College Record*, and other media widely read by educators. A general description of one of the Zajonc-Upton courses and its full syllabus can be found in Chickering, Dalton, and Stamm's *Encouraging Authenticity and Spirituality in Higher Education*. It is impossible to calculate how many curricular experiments this collaboration has inspired, given this widespread coverage of a course that arose from a transformative conversation.[13]

The potential of the conversational approach to institutional and social change does not end with inspiring others. I indicated as much early in this chapter when I recalled the experience I had years ago, sitting in that circle of rocking chairs at Highlander, where Myles Horton had hosted a transformative conversation between blacks and whites that became a wellspring of the civil

THE HEART OF HIGHER EDUCATION

rights movement of the mid-twentieth century. Some may be tempted to write off the impact of the Highlander conversations as a happy accident or an artifact of a bygone time when our society was such that simple conversation could help foment widespread change. But that would be a mistake, as we have witnessed something akin to the Highlander phenomenon as recently as November 4, 2008.

That, of course, is the date on which Barack Obama was elected president of the United States—despite the fact that he is a person of color with multicultural roots, has a name that reminds small minds of Muslim extremists, ran for office with far less experience and name recognition in national politics than his rival, and belongs to a political party famous for its uncanny ability to shoot itself in the foot. I want to explore one of the taproots of Obama's electoral success: well-structured transformative conversations. I do so not because I have delusions of grandeur about you or me achieving high office. I do so because if such conversations could help Obama get elected against very heavy odds, surely they can help you and me with the much less daunting task of seeding integrative education, even in rocky soil.

As most Americans now know, Barack Obama began his social change career as a community organizer in Chicago. We know this because in the final, critical lap of the campaign, Sarah Palin, then-governor of Alaska and candidate for vice president on the Republican ticket, mocked this aspect of Obama's credentials, saying, in effect, "Clearly, a governor and a senator know much more than a lowly community organizer about practical politics, problem-solving, and advancing a difficult agenda." Palin clearly underestimated the power of community organizing experience, principles, and practices.

After graduate school, I spent five years as a community organizer in the Washington, D.C., area. During that time, it became clear to me that conversations rightly held—the kinds of transformative conversations that are the meat and drink of every community organizer—can help create real change, sometimes massive change, in the real world. Nothing I have seen or heard over the past forty years has given me reason to change my mind.

Much has been said about Obama's innovative use of technology, which was clearly a major driver of his success. But in both politics and higher education we have become so enamored of technology that we forget about the power of those person-to-person, face-to-face "live encounters" that animate the human spirit in a way nothing else can. High tech can supplement and amplify "high touch," but it can never replace it.

How did high touch animate the Obama campaign? By means of "Camp Obama," an organizing tool grounded in transformative conversations.[14] These retreats of two or three days each, held over time in every region of the country, served as gathering places for people who were at various stages of making the Rosa Parks decision to live undivided lives. Heartsick about the decline of American democracy and the pervasive violence of our society, they came to Camp Obama for the same reason people came to Highlander: seeking a public voice to help renew our political process and reweave the tattered fabric of our common life.

The design for Camp Obama was rooted in the "public narrative" work of Marshall Ganz, lecturer in Public Policy at Harvard University's Kennedy School of Government, and an ex-community organizer.[15] In a classic model of transformative conversations, participants were first asked to tell "the story of self," the story of one's personal hurts and hopes that, as it is told and heard, helps people deepen their commitment to live undivided lives. Next they were asked to tell "the story of us," the story that connects one's personal needs and hopes to those of other people, expanding the community of congruence. Then they were asked to tell "the story of now," of what might be done at this moment to heal the hurts and pursue the hopes revealed by the first two stories.

After exploring these stories and their political implications, participants went out from Camp Obama to spread across the country and involve more and more people in similar groups until they had helped to generate a political campaign nearly unique in American history and successful by every measure: spreading a message, inspiring hope, raising record sums of money from individuals, bringing new diversity into the electoral process, getting out the vote, and winning the election against considerable odds. So the "secret" of Camp Obama—a stone tossed into the political pond that rippled out on November 4, 2008, to the 64 million people who voted Obama into office—is yet another secret hidden in plain sight: telling personal stories that are connected to our hurts and our hopes, done in a well-designed and disciplined community of discourse, can help empower us to act.

As we reflect on that fact we should remember that, prior to the last election, many of us believed that the American political pond had become so frozen over that a small stone like Camp Obama, tossed into it, would simply bounce and then lie there. We should also remember that in the 1950s, many American citizens, white and black, would have said the same thing about the chances of the Highlander conversations having any appreciable impact on achieving equality under the law for all Americans.

More than a few academics hold the same "frozen pond" belief about the structures and culture of higher education. As long as we cling to that notion, it will continue to be a self-fulfilling prophecy: the academic pond will remain frozen in its infamous resistance to change. But transformative conversations—even in relation to goals far more challenging than educational reform—have a proven capacity to help melt the ice.

Afterword

Parker J. Palmer and Arthur Zajonc

What began as a conversation between the two of us has grown into a book full of questions and explorations, probes and proposals, visions and hopes. We have sought to uncover, at least in part, the heart of higher education—that which gives learning life and grants to teaching its deepest satisfaction.

We have tried to express, perhaps with only limited success, what we take to be some of education's essential characteristics. We have drawn from the sciences to argue for the primacy of experience, relationship, and the interconnectedness of humanity and the earth. We have looked through the lenses of psychology and neuroscience to investigate the stages of human unfolding. We have evoked the spiritual and religious traditions to help us craft pedagogies of attention, equanimity, and contemplative knowing. Our greatest challenge has been to convey in discursive, linear sentences what is in truth an integrated, holistic reality.

The education of the young is one of humanity's greatest communal undertakings. Through it culture, history, science, art, values, and countless other priceless discoveries, insights, inventions, and achievements are conveyed. And at the center of it all is the human being in his or her full humanity. As Wendell Berry reminded us at the outset, it is the humanity of our students that is being shaped through a compact between teachers, students, and others in the academic community.

Education is a vital, demanding, and precious undertaking, and much depends on how well it is done. If it is true to the human being, education must reflect our nature in all its subtlety and complexity. Every human faculty must be taken seriously, including the intellect, emotions, and our capacity for relational, contemplative, and bodily knowing. An integrative education is one that offers curricula and pedagogies that employ and deploy all these faculties, delights in their interactions, and is spacious enough to allow for their creative conflict.

Values such as compassion, social justice, and the search for truth, which animate and give purpose to the lives of students, faculty, and staff, are honored and strengthened by an integrative education. But to be truly integrative, such an education must go beyond a "values curriculum" to create a comprehensive learning environment that reflects a holistic vision of humanity, giving attention to every dimension of the human self. Integrative education honors communal as well as individual values and cultivates silent reflection while encouraging vigorous dialogue as well as ethical action. The geometry of the human soul is dense with such antinomies. They are essential to our nature, and real teaching and learning must reflect that inner complexity.

The conversations we call for can only take place within a context—and the particular context required for the renewal of higher education is an integrative philosophy of education made in the image of the human being. That is why we have attempted to articulate some features of an integrative educational philosophy that can support conversations about the heart of higher education and provide a loom for weaving together diverse pedagogical methods. The ideas, insights, and actions that flow from collegial conversations will be integrative only to the extent that the conversation partners share a full and rich image of what it means to be human.

That circle of rocking chairs at the Highlander Folk School is itself a symbol of what we are calling for. The Highlander conversations were grounded in an image of the human being and the human future that was not partial but whole. Had the image been fragmented, then the conversations and their consequences would have reflected that brokenness. But the words spoken in that circle were drawn from an aquifer of human wholeness that simultaneously honored and transcended race. As a result, the actions that flowed from the Highlander conversations helped give American history a more human shape.

While we are unlikely to have the pleasure of sitting in a circle and exploring these matters with more than a few of you, we hope you will feel led to initiate such conversations with colleagues on your campus. As individuals we often reflect, understand, and act in solitude. But we thrive on what arises between us—and never more so than when we are thinking and speaking together about ideas and people for whom we care deeply. The renewal we advocate will germinate first in the soil of these caring and collegial conversations.

We believe that the current generation of educators possesses all that is needed to take on the great adventure of remaking higher education in the fullness and beauty it deserves. To those who might see our suggestions as utopian, we reply that every challenge we face as a society—social, environmental, or economic—calls for an integrative response, one that draws on our most comprehensive understanding and ethical sensibility. Only integrative answers will suffice, and only an integrative education will equip our students to meet those challenges.

Educate our students as whole people, and they will bring all of who they are to the demands of being human in private and public life. The present and future well-being of humankind asks nothing less of us.

About the Appendices

EXPERIMENTS IN INTEGRATIVE EDUCATION

Throughout this book, we have pointed toward places where integrative education can be seen in action. We wanted to offer examples of the diverse forms integrative education can take—within the classroom, across academic disciplines, beyond the classroom (for example, service learning and collaborations between academic and student affairs), and campuswide programs, often initiated by administrators. So in the fall of 2008, we invited the presenters at the 2007 conference "Uncovering the Heart of Higher Education" along with other conversation partners of ours to share stories we could use in the book—stories that illustrate both models of integrative education and a conversational strategy of change.

The result is a set of stories well worth telling. But it is by no means a comprehensive survey or sampling of what is going on in the field. There are integrative education programs galore at universities, colleges, and community colleges across the land, as witnessed by the six hundred-plus attendees at "Uncovering the Heart of Higher Education." But this book is meant to be the start of a conversation, not an encyclopedic resource guide for one, so what you will find in these Appendices is only a glimpse of what is happening. We hope these stories will spark your interest, whet your appetite, and inspire you to do your own research into strategies and models that might find fertile ground on your campus.

Appendix A

In the Classroom

KNITTING THROUGH THE HALLELUJAH

Patricia Owen-Smith, Professor of Psychology and Women's Studies, Oxford College of Emory University

Colleges can be stressful and alienating places for both students and faculty. Patricia Owen-Smith describes how she recognized and addressed her own needs to slow down and to connect more deeply with her subject and her students. By bringing music and meditation into her classroom, she helped to create a contemplative space that enriched her students' experience within and beyond the classroom.

Life in the academy for me has been consistently alienating and lonely. Initially, I interpreted this estrangement as a personal flaw, but I have come to understand that the academic world of higher education has been structured in such a way so as to normalize and promote alienation. Under the guise of academic freedom and professional autonomy, we close our classroom and office doors physically and metaphorically.

Perhaps most troubling is that our students seem to mirror these same feelings of fear, loneliness, and separation. They have little confidence in their own native intelligence and wisdom, and often distrust one another's knowledge and experiences. We as teachers have been active participants in alienating students from us and themselves, perhaps because this is the only model of teaching and learning that we know. After all, we live in a society that eroticizes individualism and often pathologizes connection and collaboration. It is not surprising that we as teachers learn very early in our careers to be skeptical, suspicious, and even fearful of a deep connection with our students.

Teachers complain about students' incessant use of cell phones. We sadly note their obsession with e-mail and instant messaging as a primary venue for communication. We bemoan their fatigue and inability to draw limits in their extracurricular activities, and we criticize their competitiveness. Nevertheless, we model these ways of being in the world. A clear reflection of our own withdrawal and disengagement is the frenetic pace with which we live our lives. Somehow I learned that the more I worked, the more important I was. I believed that the darkness under my eyes, the failure to nourish my heart, soul, and body, and the irritation and anger I harbored were signs of my commitment to my work. In spite of my genuine commitment to being the best teacher possible and giving an inordinate amount of time to pedagogical innovations, I perpetuated a cycle of madness and unhealthiness.

My recognition of this exhausting behavior and my lack of attention to the essential came rather late in my teaching career, and my attempt to correct or at least ameliorate it began with two unlikely tools in the college classroom, meditative music and contemplative practice. The introduction of music at the beginning of each class initially developed out of my own needs. Music calmed my franticness and provided time for personal contemplation prior to the work of the class. I purposely chose music that was meditative, soulful, and lyrical. As a prologue to the music each day, I urged my students to go within, be still, and listen to the self. Of course, this was also a reminder for me. We sat each day for approximately seven to nine minutes and listened to music. At first, as I rested into the beauty of the music and listened to my stillness, students fiddled with their pencils and notebooks, fidgeted in their chairs, eyed their watches, and glanced toward one another in a somewhat panicked manner, perhaps fearing that they might be stuck for a semester with a teacher who was not sound of mind!

As the semester proceeded, the students adjusted and seemed to accept their "alternative" class. I grew calmer, more reflective, and more conscious of each moment in my classes. Instead of being anxious and hurried as I entered the classroom and taught, I began to think of my class as a place of peace and comfort, and I was more willing to settle into and relish each moment with the students. I was more fully present in my life and in theirs.

Music and contemplation were my first steps toward affirming and honoring an authentic conversation with my students, but I wondered, was I expecting too much? At first, I saw little evidence of change in the students. I reminded myself that I might not know what would constitute evidence of change. Like every good social scientist I knew the difficulty in and controversy surrounding the measurement of that which may be the "unmeasurable." Of course, I could consider the effect of music and contemplative practice on such variables as grades, feedback from course evaluations, and approaches to discourse and writing. Yet, these were not the changes about which I cared so deeply. Certainly, I wanted my students to understand the principles of my discipline and to leave the classroom with a firm knowledge base in the subject area; but I also hoped that they would leave with much more. I wanted them to understand what it meant to go within for the important questions and to trust the answers they find to those questions. I wanted them to develop the ability to transcend the nuisance variables of their lives. I wanted them to feel a responsibility for other human beings and all living things and to appreciate the connections we all have with one another. I wanted them to learn how to care for their souls and the souls of others. I wanted them to know that their hearts matter and that these hearts are cherished as much as their minds. I wanted them to know my heart, not just know the words I spoke in class.

In spite of my concerns that my students were merely accommodating their teacher's oddities, I continued to play the music. I continued to urge them to practice contemplation and stillness during this music and reminded them to "go within." At the same time I began to practice silently the Tonglin, a meditative practice centered on the breath in which the one meditating breathes in the pain, crises, and sorrow of others, transforms it, and then breathes out peace, healing, and loving kindness. I consciously took in my students' unhappiness and anxiety and consciously breathed out harmony and care. Of course, my students did not know of my practice, and I did not know whether my practice of the Tonglin produced changes in the students and in the ethos of the classroom. I did know that this practice was spiritually empowering for me and that I began the class work each day with greater integrity and empathic understanding.

Over time, I learned that the music and meditative moments had an impact on many students. Some students began to ask for guidance with their contemplation and reflection. One student embarrassingly told me that she did not know how to "go within" because she believed she had no internal self, a comment I fear was representative of many students' beliefs about the internal fabric of their lives.

By midsemester several students per class would mention that they looked forward to this nine-minute period of music. Some students began to bring music from their own collections that they found inspirational and important. As we neared the end of the semester, the structure of the class had changed from a group of individuals reluctantly gathered together for study to a community of friends and partners who were creating a space of introspection, quiet, and respect for the process of study and the development of self. But it wasn't until one of the final days of the semester that I understood the importance of our time together.

To celebrate the approach of the holidays I began our day with George Frideric Handel's "Hallelujah Chorus" from the *Messiah*. While many of these students were not from a Christian tradition, they nevertheless relaxed into the beauty of Handel's most influential and enduring work. While the day was cold and rainy, the classroom was filled with the majesty and magic of the choral voices.

There was another music echoing that day and another form of the Tonglin that was practiced. Earlier in the semester our college chaplain had encouraged a small group of student knitters to knit gloves, scarves, small blankets, and hats for our community neighbors who were in need of such items for the winter. While only one of these "official knitters" was in my class, she had nevertheless persuaded others in the class to join her in these efforts.

The sound of knitting needles gently permeated the classroom air with each needle playing on the other like fingers on the ivories of a piano keyboard. And there was the gentle sound and exquisite color of boughs of yarn traveling around hands, across desks, over laps, and on the floor as the fingers of freshmen and sophomore women and men moved meditatively. Just as I was practicing the Tonglin, so were my students engaging in their own meditative practice. In the stillness of their contemplation, generosity of their spirits, and the gifts of their hands, the Tonglin was never more beautifully practiced nor the *Messiah* more clearly heard.

It has been a decade since this initial introduction of contemplative music, and I cannot envision a classroom without music. Semester after semester, I watch with delight as we take a journey together, a journey whereby we hear our souls, breathe in silence, cherish stillness, and learn from one another in the most enduring ways. Our journey is a dance, a conversation, a celebration of the heart, and a sacred moment in the process we call "education."

UNCOVERING THE HEART OF HIGHER EDUCATION: THE CONTEMPLATIVE PRACTICE FELLOWSHIP PROGRAM

Mirabai Bush, Executive Director, The Center for Contemplative Mind in Society

In this essay, Mirabai Bush describes the many ways Contemplative Practice Fellows, in diverse programs and disciplines, introduce students to contemplative practice, and how this adds depth to students' under-standing of themselves, their studies, and the world. "By encouraging contemplative ways of knowing in higher education in diverse disciplines, we can encourage a new form of inquiry and imaginative thinking to complement critical thinking, and we will educate active citizens who will support a more just and compassionate direction for society."

Imagine an architecture professor saying, "I ask my students to sit in silence and then draw a simple map of their childhood, a map of the built environment where they grew up, with their house or apartment, school, playground, city block, friend's house, corner store, grandmother's house, whatever they remember that mattered to them, and they see how the structures of a community fit together and create meaning." Bradford Grant, contemplative practice fellow in Architecture at Hampton University (now at Howard), shared this practice with us at the conference "Uncovering the Heart of Higher Education." In his course Urban and Community Design and Contemplative Environmental Design Practice, Grant uses contemplative practices such as this to help his students get to a deeper and more connected understanding of what it means to build, to create, to live a meaningful life inside a structure.

Fellow David Haskell, associate professor of biology at the University of the South, teaches a course called Food and Hunger: Contemplation and Action. As part of this course, students work with local hunger-relief organizations and learn the contemplative practices that motivate and sustain many of those who work with the hungry. With increased awareness of their own minds and emotions, Haskell reports that students are better able to process the disturbing subject matter of hunger. Without some self-knowledge of one's center, it is very hard to receive the bad news about hunger and even harder to discern what one's own response might be.

When University of Connecticut poet and professor Marilyn Nelson was offered a Contemplative Practice Fellowship and an invitation to teach at West Point during the same semester, she combined the two invitations and taught poetry and meditation to cadets who were later deployed to Iraq. They e-mailed back to her about how meditation and poetry were helping them through

THE HEART OF HIGHER EDUCATION

difficult times. One said that both he and his wife (both are Black Hawk helicopter pilots) had continued to meditate during their deployments. He said that, although military culture is in some ways the antithesis of the contemplative life, they had both found it an invaluable tool to use in a crisis, especially as officers who must show composure before their soldiers, for instance, when one of their soldiers was killed or wounded. He said he camouflaged his meditating by sitting on his cot wearing headphones: Everyone thought he was listening to music, which is cool. But his headphones were silent. He was being in the moment, thinking "here, now, here, now."

Grant, Haskell, and Nelson are just three of the 145 Contemplative Practice Fellows, a program of the Center for Contemplative Mind in Society funded by the Fetzer Institute. At 101 colleges and universities, they have been teaching courses that incorporate a range of practices, including mindfulness, lectio divina, yoga, tai chi, and others that emerge from the disciplines. Together they are designing pedagogical methods and building a body of knowledge that is formulating a new way of teaching—and of learning and knowing—that complements critical thinking and the scientific method. They are demonstrating how contemplative development opens the mind to new possibilities, cultivates wisdom through deepening one's relationship to the world, and encourages compassion and empathy through an understanding of the interconnection of all life. And at the same time, scientific research is confirming that contemplation/mindfulness develops such cross-disciplinary cognitive capacities as decision making, attention, intuitive understanding, and memory as well as emotional capacities such as self-awareness, self-management, and empathy.

A few years ago, the Dalai Lama spoke at Smith College on the challenges of higher education. Without compassion, education and knowledge can be used for destructive purposes, he said; warmheartedness gives us the ability to use everything properly that we learn in our formal education. "Education gives a person strength, and a warm heart lets a person use all their knowledge for the best. Individual compassion is the key to sustaining peace of mind and peace throughout the world. Education can guide, but the heart must lead," he said. "Worldwide we need to apply more attention to education and teach the importance of a warm heart from kindergarten through university." The Center's core message is that the way to live a life of insight and compassion and respect for interconnection is to develop a contemplative mind (and heart) *within* society, cultivated through education.

A few years ago, we initiated a new series of Contemplative Practice Fellowships for courses related to social conflict and injustice, the amelioration of suffering, and the promotion of peace. We were concerned about how many people would be interested, but we received 130 applications for the first ten of these awards. Those fellows now include Daniel Barbezat, who is teaching a course in economics at Amherst focused on an extremely timely subject, Skillful Means and the Marketplace. In this course, students use contemplative practices to examine such subjects as desire and regret and their impact on local and global market activity, a course that could have benefited some of our national economic experts.

We know that the academy changes slowly and that professors need time and support to deepen a practice and perspective that actually changes the way they teach. To encourage such change, the Center has offered retreats, cross-disciplinary meetings, national conferences, webinars, and an annual summer session at Smith College. During one summer session, Jody Ziegler, who teaches art history at Holy Cross, projected a painting on the wall and asked us to write briefly what we saw, and then she read the results. Every one was different. "What is actually there? What are you bringing to it?" she asked. "Look again. And again and again." An hour later, we were still peeling back the onion of our conditioned judgments. In her classes, her students do this for thirteen weeks.

At a meeting of Fellows in arts and architecture at a Chautauqua retreat in Boulder, we sat on Stickley wooden chairs, wrapped in quilts to keep warm as snow fell outside, and we asked these questions: What can meditation offer to the arts? How do you describe contemplative practices in arts education to others? What makes me a better contemplative teacher? Simple questions; complex answers.

We were reminded of the words of Chogyam Trungpa Rinpoche, a Tibetan lama who once taught in Boulder: "Art is based on the idea that first we see our universe very clearly and very precisely and very thoroughly."

Education systems reflect society's values; therefore, most of current American education pays little attention to the potential contributions of contemplative values and perspective, including compassion and loving kindness. But society is changing, and education can either support the status quo or prepare students for the emerging new directions. By encouraging contemplative ways of knowing in higher education in diverse disciplines, we can encourage a new form of inquiry and imaginative thinking to complement critical thinking, and we will educate active citizens who will support a more just and compassionate direction for society. At a Center conference at Columbia, Jon Kabat-Zinn, founder of the Center for Mindfulness in Medicine, Health Care, and Society, urged us to *come to our senses*, to break through to the knowing that is based on direct experience, to see with eyes of wholeness, to practice awareness of the mind as if our lives depended on it—because, he said, "in virtually every way that has any meaning, literal or metaphorical, they surely do."

BORDER CROSSING: LEADERSHIP, VALUE CONFLICTS, AND PUBLIC LIFE SYLLABUS IN SERVICE OPPORTUNITIES IN LEADERSHIP

Alma G. Blount, Director, Hart Leadership Program, Terry Sanford Institute of Public Policy, Duke University

Service Opportunities in Leadership (SOL), sponsored by the Hart Leadership Program in the Terry Sanford Institute of Public Policy at Duke University, is an intensive yearlong program for undergraduates that combines academic study, service to communities, and critical reflection. The following description gives a sense of both the philosophical framework and the content and approach of the classes offered through this program.

165

Service work is at the heart of Service Opportunities in Leadership (SOL). In a highly competitive selection process, fifteen interns a year are chosen to work with innovative organizations across the United States and around the world. SOL draws a mix of freshmen, sophomores, and juniors from a range of majors. Since 1997 "SOLsters" have traveled to Central America, Eastern Europe, and Southern Africa, as well as Albuquerque, Charlotte, Chicago, New York, Pittsburgh, and the Mississippi Delta. They have worked with a variety of community projects such as microlending initiatives, refugee support services, clinical health programs, and youth mentoring efforts.

In collaboration with their host organizations and faculty mentors, students identify community needs that would benefit from sustained study. They draft research questions, determine methods for addressing the questions, collect and analyze data, and present their findings. Throughout the summer they keep a research journal that documents what they are learning about the content and process of the research project. At the end of the summer students leave a tangible product with their community partners.

When SOL interns return to campus in the fall, they participate in a public policy research seminar that allows them to integrate what they learned in the summer with concepts of politics, policy analysis, and leadership. Students complete a Social Issue Investigation Portfolio, a research project with six component parts. One is an essay on a policy topic related to the summer placement, in which students explore what they have learned about the issue from their own research and from firsthand experience. Another is an interview with a practitioner working on the front lines of the issue. Students explore the practitioner's perspectives, comparing and contrasting them with what they have seen or read themselves. Next, students write a policy memo, in which they consider several options and make a case for which approach is the most viable. Finally, they submit a summary analysis, which provides specific suggestions for fostering the political leadership required to implement their policy recommendations. Students present their social issue

THE HEART OF HIGHER EDUCATION

research to the class for extensive critique before submitting the final portfolio.

Border Crossing: Leadership, Value Conflicts, and Public Life is the preparation course for students who plan to conduct community-based research projects in the summer through the Service Opportunities in Leadership Program or another research service-learning opportunity. Through this course students are trained in basic research methods, complete a twenty-hour service project for a local community organization, and are introduced to a leadership framework for undertaking complex problem solving work in the public arena. The course is designed to provide students with theoretical knowledge and critical reflection skills for entering other cultures to conduct research with community organizations. Setting the stage is important for the quality of the class experience. The following description on the syllabus introduces students to the central themes of the course:

> It is inevitable that you will encounter value conflicts when you enter a new culture, and some of the most important work of this course will be our mutual reflection on the meaning, uses and misuses of these conflicts. We will approach this work through our theme this semester: religion and public life. We will explore the history of how religion, politics, and public policy issues have become intertwined in the U.S. and abroad and investigate contemporary issues that represent a spectrum of viewpoints on faith and politics in our culture. The heart of the course will be a presentation of case studies that illuminate the complexities of religious values that can become either impediments to public problem solving work, or resources for its successful completion.
>
> We will study and compare several cases studies of religious and political groups—in the U.S., Europe, and the Middle East—with conflicting views about the role of religious faith in public life. The case studies will provide an avenue for grappling with the complexities of public problem-solving

work. The entire course is an exploration of leadership as the art of working productively with difficult value conflicts in groups, institutions, and social systems. Through the lens of religion and politics, we will address questions of leadership, politics, and public policy.

Participate actively in class. Pay attention to both the content and the dynamic of our class discussions, and find creative, effective ways to help deepen our conversations throughout the semester. Make your comments count. This is a safe place to express yourself honestly, so take some risks to bring fresh perspectives to our work. Quality matters far more than quantity. If your tendency is to talk a lot, try observing more, and you will be more effective. If you are shy about speaking in class, we can help you.

Whether you are writing an essay or op-ed piece, or taking a quiz on the readings, the following principles are operative. What is your analysis of the reading? What are the author's core themes and arguments? What are your own thoughts and ideas in relation to the author's viewpoint?

Your essays should be concise, well crafted, energetic pieces of writing that are a pleasure to read. Limit them to 500 words. As you write your essay, think of yourself as priming the pump for our class discussions. Use the essays to develop your own distinct voice, and remember that you are doing so in order to add something useful to our class discussions, and to enhance the quality of the learning experience for all of us.

As the semester progresses, you will be able to relate earlier readings, films, and class discussions to the texts for the current week. We are interested in your reflections about the various people and issues we study in relation to the core themes of the class: religion and public life, value conflicts, and border crossing.

The course includes a research methods component in the final weeks of the semester. "Border Crossing" is a research service-learning (RSL) Gateway course, which is part of a campuswide initiative called Scholarship with a Civic Mission.

In the final portion of the semester, you will be trained in basic community-based research methods to help you prepare for summer field work as part of the Service Opportunities in Leadership program, Scholarship with a Civic Mission, or another community-based research opportunity during the summer.

What are the highest goals of this class? Informed by scholarship and the ideas of your classmates, you will arm yourself emotionally and intellectually to enter a new culture prepared to serve and to reflect critically on your experience there. We will ask you to think deeply about how to approach the inevitable value conflicts you will face as you cross the borders of new organizations and cultures. We will ask you to examine your own religious and cultural values and preconceptions. We will challenge you to explore how you can, over time, become a fully engaged citizen of your own society. We look forward to doing this work with you.

We expect this class to stimulate and challenge each of us intellectually, emotionally and morally. We expect our work together to be both rigorous and enjoyable for all of us.

PUTTING STUDENTS FIRST: PROMOTING LIVES OF PURPOSE AND MEANING

Larry A. Braskamp, Loyola University Chicago, Lois Trautvetter, Northwestern University, and Kelly Ward, Washington State University

Braskamp and his colleagues note that for faculty and staff to "put students first," to teach to the whole student, requires "the development of the whole faculty member or staff member. Faculty need to be better recognized, evaluated, and nurtured for their contributions in meeting the holistic needs of today's college students." They report that this happens most successfully on campuses that foster informal interactions between faculty and students and campuswide conversations.

How can higher education faculty, administrators, and staff create campus environments that assist students in their learning in preparation for chosen careers and guide them in developing a sense of well-being, purpose, and individual and social responsibility? How can we help students find a sense of "calling" in life? What interventions in a college student's journey in life most effectively prepare students for disciplinary excellence, successful careers, and a meaningful life?

As we report in our book, *Putting Students First: How Colleges Develop Students Purposefully* (2006), many campuses are exploring these questions in order to examine critically the educational process and take direct steps toward preparing students for a life that encompasses a sense of purpose and meaning.

"It takes a whole campus of whole persons to develop whole students" portrays a philosophy of creating a campus that intentionally guides students in finding purpose and meaning in their lives. "Putting students first" is an important first step and the anchor of this commitment to create collaborative environments among and between faculty, student affairs professionals, and campus ministry. Based on our study of ten colleges, the starting point was that nearly everyone in the campus community agreed to focus on the question of what is best for the students. To them this meant respecting students for who they are and where they are in their life, not what and who we want them to be or only what higher education leaders think they should be in their stage of development.

These colleges defined student learning and development in terms of meaning and purpose, using a variety of words such as *vocation*, *spirituality*, or *religious development*, to convey the "good life." The key is that students' inner life is not to be separated from their outer life. Being and doing are mutually reinforcing; "who one is" represents a critical element in understanding one's goals, motivation, source of meaning, as well as the foundation of the "good life." This perspective is beautifully communicated by the provost of Villanova University, who states, "We encourage students to let their intellectual life be guided by their hearts. Students are learning and developing in college for a purpose: that is, to be of service to the world."

In the colleges we studied, faculty and staff are encouraged to be "whole persons" in their role, that is, to express their cognitive, intrapersonal, and interpersonal dimensions in their relationships with students. Relationships built on trust, respect, and openness among faculty, staff, and students are critical in fostering holistic student development. It is also easier to challenge and encourage students when rapport among students, faculty, and staff exists. To get to this point, frequent and in-depth interactions between faculty and students are necessary. Obviously the classroom is an important place for faculty and student interaction. But from the perspective of students, far more important are the informal interactions faculty have with their students in places like dining areas, residence halls, office hours, and faculty homes.

The development of the whole student requires the development of the whole faculty member or staff member. Faculty need to be better recognized, evaluated, and nurtured for their contributions in meeting the holistic needs of today's college students. Assessment must be designed and implemented to reinforce a person's development and vocation. This pertains to everyone in the community—students, staff, and faculty. The issue for the future is the extent to which the assessment practices mirror the college's mission and identity. Do a college's practices reflect an approach of "sitting beside" rather than "standing over"? Some of the implications are more faculty peer evaluations, evaluation practices that reinforce a community of persons all seeking to learn and develop themselves as human beings.

Faculty contributions to the local campus need to be sufficiently recognized if the college expects to fulfill its goals and support the personal and career development of the faculty member, the staff member, and the student. Development of faculty and staff must include vocation and the identity of the individual faculty member. Student development often employs the concept of identity, but recently vocation as a calling to lead a life that is authentic and of service to others has become a concept that has powerful implications. Vocation is also an excellent way for faculty to think about their contributions at their campus. It can motivate those of all ages, especially those with considerable experience. Faculty thinking about their own vocation will influence students in their thinking about their vocations and careers.

More recently one of us has reinterpreted and expanded this holistic development focus by incorporating a global perspective. That is, given the increasing complexity of the world and its pluralism, ethnic and religious diversity, globalization and internationalization, everyone—students, faculty, and staff—needs to adopt a new worldview that stresses how one views oneself in the world.

Developing students holistically requires the participation of everyone in the campus community, in and out of the classroom. We leave with you these reflective questions as a starting point to creating campus conversations for holistic faculty and student development:

- What is the mission and identity of your institution as it relates to fostering holistic development?
- At your institution who are the champions or leaders in guiding students in their search for meaning and purpose?
- How are faculty and staff at your institution expected to guide students intellectually, socially, civically, physically, religiously, spiritually, and morally?
- What are the salient challenges, barriers, and opportunities your institution needs to address in creating a campus environment that fosters a global holistic development?
- How do you encourage and prepare faculty to work with students in the co-curricular context at your institution?
- How is community defined at your institution? What can you and your colleagues do to cultivate an even greater sense of campus community?
- How is your campus addressing the big questions of the "good life"?

SOURCES

Larry Braskamp, Lois Trautvetter, and Kelly Ward, *Putting Students First: How Colleges Develop Students Purposefully* (Bolton, MA: Anker, 2006).

Arthur Chickering and Larry Braskamp, "Developing a Global Perspective for Personal and Social Responsibility," *Peer Review* 11 (Winter 2009), pp. 27–30.

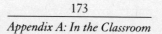

Appendix A: In the Classroom

Appendix B

Beyond the Classroom

THEME DORMS: MIXING
ACADEMICS AND COLLEGE LIFE

Sharon Daloz Parks, Senior Fellow, Whidbey Institute

Creating, learning, and teaching in a theme dorm bring home to teachers and students alike the transformative power of learning in community. As Parks points out, learning in community "changes our behavior in the world" and is what is most "vital for the future of individuals, communities and societies."

My first appointment as a teacher in American higher education was as an instructor at Whitworth College. The college had recently made a bold commitment to the education of the whole person, and David Erb, then vice president for student affairs, provided leadership in the creation of "theme dorms"—a new housing cluster of six two-story residences, each housing twenty-two students in single rooms with a common lounge and small kitchen. Each dorm was the home of a different course (the subjects rotating from year to year). Thus in each living unit, everyone took one course in common. I had the privilege of team-teaching a course within this framework—The Integration of Religion and Life. The other professor, Ronald Frase (sociology), and I (religion) held class in the dorm lounge for three hours in the afternoon, twice a week.

As a central feature of the pedagogy, we wanted to create a sense of community among the students to foster deeper learning. We put several commitments in place that students confirmed when they chose to sign up for the course, including attendance at all class sessions and participation in one social event with the others in the dorm every week. (Faculty did not typically attend the weekly social event, and the focus of this event—movie, picnic, etc.—was determined by the students.)

At the beginning of the term, we facilitated the students' discussion about how they would live together during the term. We strongly encouraged them to use a consensus process for making decisions to insure that all voices would be taken into account. We helped them consider making decisions through a consensus process, and for most of the students it was the beginning of discovering alternatives to a simple "majority rule" process.

Within this framework, the course proceeded as any other academic course—readings, faculty presentations, discussions, term papers. The delight for me as an instructor was the awareness that as we raised significant questions in class, the discussion could naturally extend beyond the class period and throughout the week, as everyone in the living context was working the same set of questions.

The course attracted some of the most outstanding student leaders on campus. The course also attracted others such as John, a student who was very bright and articulate but not a high-performing student nor part of the established social swim. He prided himself on being "outside" the conventional circle, yet was a bit awed to find himself in this social group when he did not regard himself as "their type." He went out of his way to test the tolerance of the group.

Over the course of the term he took off some of his armor, as it were, became an integral part of "the crowd," a high-performing student, and a primary contributor to the overall welfare of the group.

A few years later, looking back on that experience among others, John reflected: "Whitworth wants you to become a particular kind of person." With some trepidation we asked, "What kind of person?" He replied, "A real one." Another student, now a faculty member herself, reflecting on the same theme dorm course, remarked: "In the Religion and Life theme dorm, we all watched John move through a transformative process, and we learned that transformation was possible for all of us."

As such, that outcome was never stated in the syllabus, but it remains one of my most formative and gratifying experiences across forty years of being a professor. It was a pivotal experience in my discovering the power of the social group in the learning process. Surely there is knowledge that can be acquired through independent study. But the transformational learning that is now vital for the future of individuals, communities, and societies—learning that changes our behavior in the world—is most effectively learned in community. It is difficult to adopt new ideas that require a change in behavior if it will leave me bereft of belonging in meaningful terms. If, however, I have access to a sociality—a network of belonging—that shares my new insight and understanding, my learning is more apt to become truly formative of my self and my worldview.

Communities of shared inquiry and discovery, particularly those that are sustained over a significant period of time, play a key role in transformational learning throughout adulthood. Most recently, I have witnessed the power of "a learning community" while teaching both in a nine-month cohort-based executive leadership program for mid-career business executives at Seattle University and in a leadership retreat cycle at the Whidbey Institute in which professionals from across sectors gather as a cohort once each season for an entire year. But it must be observed that especially in the twenty-something years of emerging adulthood, while access to a good mentor can be valuable, participation in "a mentoring community" serves a yet more profound formation of orienting lifelong commitments. Young adults are given access to "dreams" by intention or default—and the value assumptions that shape those dreams will be determined by the socialities that undergird them. Higher education at its best provides access to mentoring communities—whether they are formed in a classroom, seminar, chemistry lab, residence hall, or on the soccer field—in which young, emerging adults can engage the big questions of our time and experience worthy ways of thinking and being, becoming adept in practices of mind, heart, and hand that serve the common good.

This consciousness of the role of the social world in the formation of the intellect is a critical feature in the great adventure of teaching and learning. At this threshold time in history, if we are going to encourage the formation of the citizenship and leadership that is now required, we must pay close attention to the social contexts in which we learn and teach.

STIRRING STUDENTS' INTELLECTUAL PASSIONS: THE LIBBY RESIDENTIAL ACADEMIC PROGRAM

Deborah J. Haynes, Professor and former Chair of Art and Art History at the University of Colorado, Boulder

This model interdisciplinary arts and residential program introduces students to the arts, going beyond technique and engaging their passions. Using contemplative practice, the program invites students into an experiential relationship to the arts.

Having had six years of intensive experience as a department chair in two academic departments within two universities (Women's Studies and Art and Art History), I was asked by the dean of our College of Arts and Sciences in 2003 to organize and direct a new interdisciplinary program in the arts. In developing the program, I worked closely with the department chairs of Art and Art History, Theatre and Dance, Film Studies, and the dean of the College of Music. This has been my most rewarding administrative service, as it has given me the opportunity to explore and design an integrated arts education in a large corporate state university.

The Libby Residential Academic Program (LRAP or Libby RAP) offers an interdisciplinary curriculum in the visual and performing arts for first-year students and sophomores in the College of Arts & Sciences at the University of Colorado, Boulder. The program's curriculum and co-curricular activities are intended to enhance students' appreciation of and direct experience in all of the arts. I believe that it is a model of what integrative education can be.

Much has been written about teaching and learning in the arts, especially about the crucial role of experience and the need to help students cultivate an experimental perspective that is actively curious about the world and our creative responses to it. Courses therefore combine inquiry and experience as the program seeks to stir the students' intellectual passions. The Libby RAP is also strongly conceptual, rather than being based in techniques or materials. What we seek to teach is *an approach* to the visual and performing arts. Rather than focusing on techniques, materials, or traditions per se, we ask the students, "What are your ideas and what are your passions? What vehicles will most help you to develop your ideas?" Most students find this a challenging and exciting kind of inquiry.

Contemplative practice is a central element of the program. Because the University of Colorado is a public research university, I believe it is crucial to explain clearly to university administrators, faculty, staff, parents, and students exactly what contemplative education is and what it is not. These questions arise because some people are concerned that it might involve, however tacitly, religious education that is inappropriate in a secular state university.

Broadly understood, contemplative practices are methods to develop concentration, deepen understanding and insight, and cultivate awareness and compassion. As such, contemplative or mindfulness practices can have a profound impact on a student's experience both in college and beyond. Techniques that LRAP faculty use include formal bowing, sitting, breath awareness, simple yoga postures, mindful walking, and writing. Specifically, teaching students techniques of awareness, concentration, and means of disciplining their attention is absolutely essential in our era of fragmentation, ever-increasing speed, multitasking, and continuously interrupted attention.

The program has grown from an initial cohort of 80 students in 2004 to nearly 300 during 2008–09. In its first year LRAP offered fourteen courses in the disciplines of art history, dance, film studies, music appreciation, studio arts, and theatre. During the 2008–09 academic year, we offered students forty-four courses in these areas, along with economics, nutrition, and religion and cultural history. Libby RAP's small seminar and studio courses (with 15–25 students per class) create a close intellectual and artistic community, and students usually take one or two courses in the program each semester. Most courses fulfill university core requirements, while others are prerequisites for majoring in the academic departments of art and art history, theatre and dance, and film studies. The curriculum offers students an ideal starting point for a major in any of these departments, although students from any major in the sciences, social sciences, and humanities may participate in the program. The program is funded through several sources, including a yearly program fee paid by students and support from Housing and the College of Arts and Sciences.

Residents are introduced to the diversity of the arts through opportunities to see exhibitions and performances, meet artists of both regional and national stature, and view films of historical and contemporary significance. Other activities include field trips to regional arts organizations, as well as to events held both on- and off-campus in the Denver metropolitan area. One highlight last year was taking a large group to see Cirque du Soleil. Students talked about the performance for weeks afterwards. We also organize other activities that are more directed toward community building. Such activities have included an overnight ski trip into the Colorado Rocky Mountains, visiting Denver's largest amusement park with a group of nearly forty students, and attending Denver Nuggets basketball games. At the end of each semester we sponsor a celebration of the arts, which has grown to be so popular that there is standing room only in the 3,000-square-foot basement that houses our dance and performance space and art studio.

One of the most visible markers of the program's success has been the development over three years of a series of murals in the large lobby of Libby Hall, which houses over 400 students and has one of the finest dining facilities on campus. Hundreds of resident and nonresident students traverse the lobby each day. These murals, which were designed and painted by students under the guidance of artist Tyler Alpern, have helped to create an atmosphere of aesthetic beauty and creativity that captivates all who enter Libby Hall.

SERVICE LEARNING: INSPIRED BY A STUDENT

Marshall C. Eakin, Director of the Ingram Scholars Program, Professor of History, Vanderbilt University

A student's passion and commitment opens a professor's eyes to the possibilities in service learning. The program they develop becomes a learning and life-expanding experience for the students, the communities they serve, and the faculty involved in the program. "Service-learning is the most powerful teaching method I have ever employed in my 27 years of college teaching.... When service-learning works, the communities benefit from the work and the students learn valuable and powerful real-life lessons that make their academic work come to life."

In the spring of 1996, Rachel McDonald appeared at my office door and introduced herself. She had just come back from working with Alternative Spring Break (ASB) in Lima, Peru. Inspired by her experience, she hungered for some way to connect her commitment to community service with the rigorous academic curriculum at Vanderbilt. Her advisor, one of my colleagues in the History Department, knew of my work with ASB and my own research and teaching on Latin America, so he sent Rachel to speak with me. When she first sat down and starting speaking so passionately of her experience and the need for classes that combined service and learning, I thought, "Who is this woman, and what kind of wild idea is this?" The more she talked, however, the more she persuaded me that this idea of combining community service and a Latin American studies class might work—and might actually be a good idea. Little did I know!

At about the same time, I was serving on a committee to evaluate service and volunteerism on the Vanderbilt campus. This committee included some of the most inspiring students I have ever met as well as Dwight Giles, a faculty member at Peabody and a national leader in the movement to promote service learning. I also had recently met Sharon Shields, a professor at Peabody, who had been teaching service-learning courses for decades. These students, Dwight, and Sharon made me aware of service learning, what it is, and how to do it.

Inspired and assisted by Rachel, I began scouting out the possibilities of doing a course in Lima, Peru, but we soon decided to concentrate on Chile instead. In her sophomore year, Rachel was awarded an Ingram Scholarship and went to Chile in the summer of 1997 to scout out locations for the course. She worked with one of my former students, Will Clark, a Latin American Studies major who had set up his own program to bring study abroad and service groups to Chile. Through their work, we arranged to teach a Maymester course (a four- to five-week study abroad program immediately following the spring semester) in northern Chile in the summer of 1998. That summer, twelve students and I, along with Rachel as my teaching assistant, spent four weeks in a small town of about 300 inhabitants in the northern Atacama Desert. We lived in and worked with a residential vocational high school, building a laundry, tutoring students, all the while doing an intensive three-credit course, The Historical Roots of Contemporary Chilean Social Problems. I came back from Chile profoundly moved by Rachel's commitment to service, a commitment rooted in deeply held religious beliefs. Her strong moral compass and her compassion for her fellow human beings forced me to take a hard look at my own core beliefs and commitments.

I was inspired by the success of the course and wanted to use the same approach to serve my own community and enable students to participate who could not afford the several thousand dollars and a month away for the Maymester. This led me to team teach a course with Bill Partridge, an anthropologist in the Human and Organizational Development program at Peabody. Our course, Latin America, Latinos, and the U.S., combined a rigorous academic curriculum with student work and projects in the rapidly growing Hispanic community in Nashville.

A convergence of fortunate circumstances then turned my attention back to service learning in Latin America. First under the leadership of Chancellor Gordon Gee and then Nick Zeppos, Vanderbilt began sustained efforts to promote the international dimensions of teaching, research, and service at Vanderbilt. In 2005, the newly created Vanderbilt International Office (VIO) under the leadership of Joel Harrington organized a committee to plan innovative new international programs for Vanderbilt. After a year of extended conversations, this committee recommended the creation of an international service-learning program, an experience that would be unique in its combination of study abroad and service. Through the Vanderbilt Initiative for Scholarship and Global Engagement (VISAGE), each spring students take a three-credit course that is mainly an academic curriculum with some community service. The course prepares students—academically and logistically—to go abroad for a month during the summer to do community service and a one-credit academic course integrated with the service work. We then strongly encourage the students to take a seminar in the fall to do research and write a paper about some aspect of their experience.

Last fall we recruited nearly forty students for three programs in Nicaragua, South Africa, and Australia. The Nicaragua program was one of the great teaching experiences of my life. Our group spent the spring semester learning about Nicaraguan history, politics, culture, and society and doing service with the Hispanic community in Nashville. We then spent four weeks in Managua working with the Manna Project doing service work, mainly with young children and teenagers, in everything from computer literacy to working with children with disabilities to sports programs. The students came away from the experience deeply moved, inspired to continue with their service work, their Spanish language training, and their interest in Latin America.

I hope that service learning has helped—and will continue to help—change the lives and career choices of my students. It has certainly changed my life. Service learning is the most powerful teaching method I have ever employed in my 27 years of college teaching. The combination of academics and experience provides students with a learning experience that is much more powerful than any traditional, classroom-based course. And it is a reciprocally beneficial process for the communities and the students. When service learning works, the communities benefit from the work, and the students learn valuable and powerful real-life lessons that make their academic work come to life. In addition, students gain international experience, cultural awareness, leadership skills, and (in the case of Nicaragua) they improve their Spanish-speaking ability.

My experience in service learning has made me a more committed and effective teacher. It has fundamentally redirected my teaching and my research—all of this due to the inspiration from Rachel and other students. Rachel's profound belief in the need to serve has inspired me since I met her, and continues to inspire me still. I am so lucky she walked into my office that spring day.

UNDER THE ARCOIRIS: MAKING DREAMS COME ALIVE

Judy Goodell and Joan Avis, Professors, Counseling Psychology Department, School of Education, University of San Francisco

Project Yucatán, a community-based grassroots educational project, brings the University of San Francisco's motto "Educating hearts and minds to change the world" into being. Through this program, the learners, teachers, and community changed as they experienced the power of integrative education.

The fourteen Mayan youth looked radiant, dressed in their finest clothes. A week earlier, they had stood proudly among the July 2008 class of graduates from COBAY, their regional high school. This evening their town celebrated what they had accomplished. The blessing in the church and the fiesta for students and their parents acknowledged that these youth had done what most of the town's youth cannot—they achieved a high school education.

Three years earlier, these same youth—too poor to afford the pens, uniforms, and exams required for participation in public education—would not have been able to continue in school. Personal dreams dissolved as they headed toward limited available work opportunities. Education for rural youth is a major problem, as parents juggle the need for the income working youth provide with a desire for their children to be educated. In Tekit, approximately 85 percent of all students leave school by grade six. Most end up in lifetime work in the low-paying *guayabera* garment industry, in the fields, or in the few shops in town.

The story of what happened to change the course of these students' lives is a story about the power of integrative education as we defined and experienced it. It is the story of what unfolded in Tekit, a town approximately one hour from the colonial city of Mérida, Yucatán, Mexico.

We, the storytellers, Judy Goodell and Joan Avis, are professors in the Counseling Psychology Department at the University of San Francisco. Long disturbed by the history of oppression that characterized the haciendas, Avis obtained property containing the remnants of an old hacienda and the ancient Mayan site of Ukum. While hoping ultimately to restore it into a learning center, she approached the local government of Tekit and asked what was needed. The mayor's answer was swift: "Help educate our children and help us diversify employment opportunities." Thus Project Yucatán, a community-based grassroots educational project, was created, and Siyan Ka'an ("where the sky is born" in Mayan) became its first program.

The program was designed to meet the educational needs and development of the whole person. Run by volunteer faculty, graduate students, and staff from USF's School of Education, it offered four levels of integrative service. First, scholarships funded the costs of school and subsidized families for wages "lost" due to the youth attending school. Second, a two-week daily intensive personal growth and development program was delivered at the hacienda each summer for three years. Third, an Internet café was established on the town plaza as a collaboration between the mayor's office and

Project Yucatán, with computers donated by USF. Fourth, ongoing personal support to students and families was provided through e-mail and periodic visits throughout the year.

The motto of USF is "Educating hearts and minds to change the world." We believed from the outset that education of the mind, heart, and spirit must unfold concurrently for meaningful change to occur. Yet even we were amazed at what began to take shape as teachers and learners opened themselves to deep engagement in the circles of each other's lives.

Siyan Ka'an began in the summer of 2005 with ten boys and ten girls who were selected for having high potential but limited resources. The summer program added personal growth and development activities. During summer 2005 the students discovered that learning could be enjoyable. Each day a truck picked students up at the town plaza for transport to the hacienda land. Students, many of whom were hungry, received two meals while there. Work was done on tables under the trees or on the porch of the unrestored Casa Principal. USF graduate volunteers delivered the program, directed by Avis and Goodell. Students were taught photography, art, and poetry. None had previously held a paintbrush; only one had used a camera. They received lessons in English, public speaking, goal setting, gaining confidence, assertiveness, and self-esteem. They wrote in journals and filled out application forms. They took field trips to nearby Mayan cultural sites including Uxmal, Mayapan, and Chichen Itza where trilingual guides taught them about their heritage. Most importantly, they began to dare to dream and to believe that life might be different for them and their families.

Initially Siyan Ka'an was planned to be a one-year program of summer session followed by scholarships for the tenth grade. It quickly became clear that the students needed additional mentoring and support because the cultural pictures of how life for young Mayans was supposed to unfold was so deeply engrained. These youth could visualize a dream, but they did not know how to formulate the steps for making it come true. Images of failure, acceptance, and passive resignation were strong. The program evolved and shifted as we came to better understand their needs.

As a result, we decided that Siyan Ka'an would follow the original group through to graduation.

The summer 2006 program increased the focus on personal dreams, identification of necessary skills, resources, and potential challenges. Gender-based counseling groups for boys and girls provided additional support. We discovered how students viewed obstacles—one major bump in the road was enough to create perceptions of total failure. When failure on a single exam caused one girl to temporarily quit school and the program, we instantly began a major focus on strategies for overcoming obstacles. Summer 2006 ended with students participating in a creative three-hour obstacle course set up at the hacienda—finding things, going over, around, and through difficulties, being "interviewed" for jobs and rejected, but finding acceptance at a second try.

Summer of 2007 focused on English, public speaking, writing, and development of plans for manifestation of current life dreams. Summer field trips to Universidad Autonoma de Yucatán (UADY) and Universidad Technologia Metropolitana (UTM) allowed students to explore campuses and learn about the national CENEVAL exam all must pass in their area of interest to enter a public university. Newly formed collegial relationships at UADY opened further possibilities of higher education for students.

The CENEVAL exam loomed as a huge obstacle. Students would be competing with affluent youth from all over Mexico, youth who had grown up with newspapers, travel, knowledge of English, and multiple enrichment opportunities. A team of student leaders from UADY provided Saturday-afternoon tutoring sessions in Tekit. Scholarships were offered to Siyan Ka'an students to attend a two-week exam preparation course held at UADY.

After all fourteen students passed the exams to graduate from high school, twelve took the CENEVAL with hopes of entering higher education. These students now have entered UADY, UTM, or teacher preparation programs in majors such as accounting, dentistry, engineering, biology, teaching, and tourism. One completed beautician's school and another entered a government program where he is teaching Spanish to Mayan-speaking children.

Several themes emerged as we reflect on what we have learned through involvement in Project Yucatán. In participatory integrative projects, process and outcomes continually interact and inform one another. Flexibility is essential, as new understandings of student needs lead to program modifications and changes. Patience is important, as minds, hearts, and souls learn and grow at different rates and in different ways. Multidimensional, enjoyable learning experiences are essential to keep students engaged, particularly when work and home responsibilities weigh heavily. Delivering an integrative educational program in a different culture requires a willingness to participate in community ritual events and story making; it is with curiosity, joy, and gratitude that we have done so. It is part of the rich legacy of *our* own learning. Integrative participatory education is reciprocal. When one heart, mind, and spirit connects to another, both become teacher and learner, and both are changed.

PHILADELPHIA UNIVERSITY: WHERE PHYSICAL EDUCATION MAKES A PLAY FOR CIVIC EDUCATION

Tom Schrand, Interim Dean, School of Liberal Arts, and Aurelio Valente, Assistant Dean, Student Development, Philadelphia University

At the Philadelphia University, a team of faculty, administrators, and community leaders met to introduce an aspect of civic engagement and service learning to their physical education requirement. Thus through SERVE-101, the University lays the groundwork for students to become informed, engaged, and active citizens.

As part of its commitment to integrative learning, Philadelphia University has recently taken steps to develop the civic engagement of its students. Service-learning opportunities are already a feature of some of our core curriculum courses, but we wanted to create a more structured pathway to help our students develop into active citizens and to build stronger ties with our local neighborhood, the East Falls section of northwest Philadelphia. After completing a three-year Integrative Learning Project grant from the Carnegie Foundation for the Advancement of Teaching and the Association of American Colleges and Universities (AAC&U), we began shifting our integrative efforts from the classroom curriculum to the community around us.

As a first step, we attended the AAC&U Greater Expectations Institute with a campus team selected to focus on civic engagement and service learning. In addition to the representatives from our core curriculum leadership, we also brought our assistant dean for student development, a member of our architecture faculty to represent the university's various professional majors, and the executive director of the East Falls Development Corporation, who could help us coordinate service-learning projects in our Philadelphia neighborhood.

During our work at the institute, we learned that our student development representative had already begun preliminary discussions with our dean of students and the director of athletics to consider adding civic engagement to our physical education requirements. Our time together at the institute allowed us to think creatively and collectively about the possibilities of using the parameters of a PE course (contact time, credit hours) to introduce students to civic engagement at the beginning of their university experience. Our collaboration resulted in the development of SERVE-101, a course designed to help students realize the reciprocal nature and responsibilities of citizenship for the individual and community through both practical applications and critical reflection.

In this course, students will have the option to work within an area of personal interest and passion such as, but not limited to, (1) advocacy and human rights, (2) children and youth, (3) community development and revitalization, (4) education and literacy, and (5) hunger and homelessness. Within their chosen area, students will explore the impact of service on the community and analyze the dynamics of meaningful social action aimed at addressing social inequities. This intentional service, reflection, understanding, and action model is designed to help students evolve from "volunteers," defined as those who are well-intentioned but ill-informed about the complexity of social issues, to "ethically responsible citizens" within the active citizenship continuum.

Since our students typically fulfill their physical education (PE) graduation requirements in their first two years, this offers an opportunity to lay the groundwork for an intentional and progressive approach to community engagement and citizenship that would build over four levels of curricular and co-curricular activities. The four levels include civic engagement activities as new students transition to the institution, civic engagement with a social action component as students progress through the active citizenship model in conjunction with the core curriculum, and then service-learning initiatives in both the upper-level core curriculum and the professional programs. This model shaped the development of the new SERVE-101 course and connected it with our new strategic plan that calls for the promotion of a "signature pedagogy" based on experiential and applied education in the form of intentional and educationally focused collaboration between academic affairs and the student life division.

When this proposal was brought through the approval process, the university curriculum committee recommended that students be permitted to enroll in the SERVE course up to four times: once to meet the physical education graduation requirement, as originally intended, and as many as three additional times as a free elective. The new course can also serve as a linked course credit, in which students connect their SERVE projects with the learning objectives of an accompanying course, following a "3+1" model, commonly referred to as a fourth-credit option. Participating in the fourth-credit option helps students find a deeper understanding of the content of the linked course through real world application of what they are learning. By repurposing requirements and credits already built into the curriculum, the academic affairs and student life leaders at Philadelphia University have found a strategy that allows us to promote our students' civic education in a way that is both logistically practical and developmentally effective.

Looking back over the successful outcome of this process, Marion Roydhouse, the acting vice president for academic affairs, who was part of the team that initiated this project and participated in the curricular discussions about the proposed new course, remarked: "We were impressed by how responsive the campus community was to this idea. Not only did the physical education department give their full support, but the members of our university curriculum committee were quick to see the parallels between physical education and civic education in terms of our students' overall development. This turned out to be a very direct and painless way to introduce civic engagement as a formal part of the university's curriculum."

BRINGING CONVERSATION INTO THE ESSENCE OF TEACHING: MAKING MEANINGFUL CONNECTIONS

Leslie Davenport, Clinical Faculty and Integrative Psychotherapist, Institute for Health & Healing

The Institute for Health & Healing offers a clinical program in Integrative Medicine—integrating their academic education with experiential learning: "The premise is that caregivers are better able to make meaningful connections with patients and to each other when they have greater awareness of and insight into their own personal responses and feelings."

The Institute for Health & Healing offers a clinical education program in Integrative Medicine. It is an interdisciplinary model, with students in nursing, psychology, massage, harp, and chaplaincy working together as a team with patients in the hospital who have a variety of medical and surgical conditions. The programs are designed with a whole-person philosophy and approach. The guided imagery/expressive arts and chaplaincy tracks in particular work in conjunction with graduate schools. Counseling psychology and seminary students integrate their academic education with experiential learning.

Once students are grounded in the basics of their discipline for a sound therapeutic encounter, they are encouraged to bring an open mind and heart into their work with patients, realizing that who they are with each person is as important, in some cases more important, as what they say or do. This approach maintains a deep relationship to the beautiful mystery of being human while developing professional competencies within the ethical standards of their field. Therapeutic presence is the atmosphere for attending to the person's pain and vulnerability, while engaging their inner resiliency and wholeness.

The learning model for this program is based on action/reflection, bringing conversation into the essence of teaching. As students reflect on their clinical experiences, they are asked to notice their impressions of themselves and the patient, including

- the need that arose from the patient's physical/emotional/spiritual pain
- the patient's strengths and resources
- the most salient moment in the encounter
- what was communicated nonverbally
- what the practitioner and the patient moved away from, and why
- what feelings and impulses arose in the practitioner
- what the practitioner learned from the experience

These impressions are shared with a community of faculty and peers through case presentations. Everyone is encouraged to listen deeply and add their reflections. Other students and faculty might inquire why the practitioner responded to the patient in a particular moment, or share what they would have done if they had been there. Someone might shine a light on an aspect of the encounter that was not explored. Through these reflective conversations there is an emphasis toward increasing the practitioner's capacity for therapeutic presence, not simply honing skills.

While there are clinical guidelines, high regard is given to the uniqueness of every encounter. Just as there are no two snowflakes that are the same, neither are there two patients with the same needs, even if they share the same diagnosis. Entering the field of the unknown, with awareness, is where the greatest learning takes place. Even though we offer medically based clinical education, "What is healing?" is not taught in the program—it is asked. And it is asked freshly with each encounter.

This learning model also interfaces with the medical system at large. The vision is not only to bring this therapeutic presence into work with patients and families, but also to bring the quantitative practices of medicine into partnership with the qualitative experiences of the practitioners.

One example of how this is being done is through Schwartz Rounds, a forum where all levels of medical center staff, including physicians, nurses, residents, students, social workers, unit clerks, and administrators, come into conversation with each other and reflect on important emotional and social issues that arise in caring for the patients and themselves. The premise is that caregivers are better able to make meaningful connections with patients and to each other when they have greater awareness of and insight into their own personal responses and feelings.

These learning experiences at the Institute for Health & Healing loop back into the university settings, as students bring their experiences into oral and written presentations at their schools as part of their requirements for graduation.

Appendix C

Administrative and Campuswide Initiatives

THE VP IS IN: BEING VISIBLE AND AVAILABLE

Jon Dalton, Associate Professor of Higher Education and Director of the Hardee Center for Leadership and Ethics at Florida State University

How can administrators reach out to students at a large institution? In a seemingly simple gesture, Jon Dalton found an innovative way to become available and to connect with students at Florida State University.

One of the greatest challenges to integrating learning in large institutional settings in higher education is creating an environment that enables students to feel noticed and included. When students feel connected and bonded to an institution's culture, they are likely to describe their school as "friendly," and students who perceive themselves to be in a friendly environment are more likely to invest themselves in activities and behaviors that promote academic engagement and success.

What are the circumstances and conditions that encourage personal connection and belonging in college? Human scale is one important factor. Institutions with small enrollments have the advantages of more frequent face-to-face contact and a more intimate scale of community. But large size does not have to be an insurmountable barrier in creating a sense of personal connection and belonging. There are a variety of ways to personalize the environment.

For example, while serving as vice president for student affairs at Florida State University I continued a tradition that I had begun many years earlier as dean of students at Iowa State University. Almost every Wednesday I would sit at a table on the FSU Student Union plaza beside the many student clubs, bake sales, ticket raffles, and vendors who showed up for the popular student Flea Market Day. It was my custom to bring a pad of paper, a cell phone, and two plastic chairs to my table where I displayed a large sign that announced in big letters, "The VP Is In." The idea came to me from reading Peanuts cartoons and seeing Lucy sitting at her "psychiatrist" booth.

When I first began this practice, students would walk by and glance at me, sometimes smiling, but seldom stopping. I could see the questions in their eyes: who *is* this old guy and what is he doing here? But as the weeks went by and I became a more regular fixture of the Wednesday Flea Market, students would stop by to say hi or to ask me what I was doing there. I told them who I was and that I was interested in meeting and helping students with their problems.

There is something about a flea market table that works for college students. Perhaps it is because it is located on their turf and they feel free to walk up or walk away. Perhaps the idea of a college administrator sitting alone in a bustling student flea market just seems so funky that it was "cool" to them. I am sure there were some sweet students who stopped by to talk to me just out of a sense of pity for a guy wearing a tie who was trying so hard.

As the weeks slipped into months, students would often be waiting for me at my table upon my arrival with a variety of complaints, problems, or stories to share about something special that had happened to them, or sometimes, they just wanted to say hi. Some students would park themselves in my "office" chair for the entire hour or until they were chased off by other waiting students. Here they shared problems that I rarely heard about in my big office in the administration building. They talked to me about campus food, academic advising, financial aid, college red tape, insults, grades, games, professors, passions, and, of course, parking problems. They invited me to events, tried to sell me all sorts of things, pressed me about my life and work, advised me on all sorts of topics, and shared their wisdom on how to run the university . . . and the world.

Often I could do no more on Wednesdays than listen to their problems but usually I could at least try to advise them on what to do or, best of all, call someone on my cell phone and get their problem quickly solved. Always, always they were grateful that I listened and tried to help.

It was important for me to be there, to be at my table on Wednesdays as consistently as possible. Some Wednesdays when it rained or was chilly I sat alone at my table with the other vendors who braved the elements. Doing something this crazy can easily be seen as a gimmick but persistence and regularity can make it authentic. In my work with college students I learned that few things seem as reassuring to young people as just being there.

Over the years that I did "The VP Is In," I observed how this simple symbolic act helped to create a more positive student culture. I never tried to measure the impact scientifically; I didn't have to. Often students would tell me that they saw me at the Flea Market and that they liked my being there . . . even if they never stopped to talk to me. I think, in some small way, my presence helped to convey to students a feeling that the university cared about them and would go to great lengths to reach them. Perhaps being at the Flea Market on Wednesdays helped to create a real and symbolic human connection that made this big university feel a little smaller for students.

Council of Elders: President and Faculty/Staff Relationships

Thomas Coburn, President Emeritus, Naropa University, Colorado

Even at a university committed to contemplative education, turmoil can create chasms between administration and faculty. Here President Emeritus Thomas Coburn describes a unique process that helped the college community to cross barriers and build trust between administration and faculty.

Toward the end of my second year as president of Naropa University, the university experienced one of those institutional convulsions that periodically seize virtually every college and university. The particulars of the Naropa case are not important. Suffice it to say that it was cut from the same cloth as other events that occur frequently in higher education: a student protest over the denial of tenure to a popular teacher; a rift between faculty and administration over a contentious policy; a sit-in over investment of the university endowment; turmoil over diversity issues; and so on. These episodes, like this one at Naropa, are often very public and serve as a kind of lightning rod, drawing a response from the community that is far larger than the specific issue, laced with emotional distress over previously latent issues and a nastiness that is surprising and often hugely disruptive.

I was particularly startled by such a convulsion happening at Naropa, because our signature activity—what had drawn me to Naropa—is "contemplative education," a synthesis of liberal education and contemplative practice that the university's mission statement describes as recognizing "the inherent goodness and wisdom of each human being" and embracing "the richness of human diversity with the aim of fostering a more just and equitable society and an expanded awareness of our common humanity." I asked myself, What has happened here? Beyond the particulars of this crisis, what might I do to cultivate a greater sense of trust and equanimity within the community?

I mused on this matter after the semester ended, the particular crisis wound down, and the summer wore on. Slowly I realized that there is broadly distributed within higher education a practice that might be adapted to a new purpose. Virtually all colleges and universities have a committee, elected by the faculty, to review tenure and promotion cases. In my experience, those who are elected to this committee by their peers are not necessarily the best scholars, the best teachers, or the campus politicians. Rather, they are the individual faculty members who are the most trusted by their peers. What would happen, I wondered, if I asked the entire community to identify the most trusted individuals in our midst and asked them to constitute a Council of Elders, which could serve as a symbol of communal trust, which might then spill over into the broader community?

Working with my senior diversity officer, Suzanne Benally, I did just that, seeking counsel from all faculty, staff, and students. About 120 individuals were named, an encouraging number. We then invited the eight most frequently named faculty and staff to come together to constitute such a Council. Communities like the Native Americans have a familiar sense of what *Elder* means, passed down over generations. But the Naropa Elders had to create a role for themselves. For the better part of a year, we met about monthly to discuss what the role of the Council might be.

Gradually, and with the assistance of an organizational consultant who was himself a Native American, the Elders came to a sense of their place in the university. They became the eyes and the ears of the institution, alert to concerns in the community that lie just under the surface, often eluding the governance structure. The Elders themselves have no place in the organizational hierarchy, thus occupying a fertile, liminal ground. They do not take on policy questions, and they do not vote or refer issues to other, conventional committees. They frequently hold listening circles throughout the community, the details of which are held in strict confidence, but whose themes find their way into the monthly conversations that my senior diversity officer and I have with them, usually over dinner.

Appendix C: Administrative and Campuswide Initiatives

The Council of Elders sees itself as having an "outward" face, attentive to the concerns of the community, and an "inward" face, attentive to the concerns of the president. They recognize the enormous challenge of serving as a university president, and they offer me their counsel in deep, personal ways that is not possible for members of my senior administration. As the culture of the Council has deepened, I have come to have absolute, unqualified trust in these individuals. In the aggregate, they provide me with an experience I can only describe as the safest space I have known in forty years in higher education.

Naropa's culture has changed a lot over the three years since the Council of Elders began. It is substantially less fractious, less volatile, more recognizably contemplative. I cannot, of course, claim that this is the direct result of having a clearly identified Council of Elders. But I believe it has played an important part. After one of our monthly meetings, which had been a particularly poignant, emotionally open, and healing one, Suzanne asked me: "Do you realize how fortunate you are, the only college president in the country other than presidents of tribal colleges to have a group like the Council of Elders to work with you and the community?" I could only beam with gratitude.

PRESIDENT AND FACULTY DINNERS: OPPORTUNITIES FOR CONVERSATIONS AND RELATIONSHIPS TO FLOURISH

Veta D. Goler, Arts and Humanities Division Coordinator, Associate Professor of Dance, Spelman College

At Spelman College, President Beverly Tatum and faculty members have come together to create President and Faculty Dinners, a space for open and honest exchange among the faculty and the president. The effort has led to a more expansive and supportive environment for faculty and has changed faculty interactions with each other and their students and stimulated "ideas about innovative curricular and co-curricular efforts that promise to enhance the community's ability to embrace multiple ways of knowing and being."

Spelman's history as a southern, black women's college of Christian origins has shaped a culture for the institution in which politeness and deference often prevent direct, honest interaction—especially in the presence of opposing viewpoints. In addition, diversity among Spelman students, faculty, and staff is often overlooked, and a Christian, heterosexual, African American norm is presumed. Where possible, many individuals who fall outside of this norm seem to feel more comfortable keeping their differences hidden. Discussions between President Beverly Daniel Tatum and Spelman faculty members about these issues raised two guiding questions: What would help faculty members interact with each other more directly and honestly? How can we make Spelman a safe space for people to be open about who they are?

In an effort to address these questions and support institutional culture change, President Tatum began hosting a series of dinners in which faculty members have open, honest dialogue—largely about themselves. Through exercises, stories, and dialogues on topics and issues of identity, these Dinner and Dialogue sessions are building community among faculty members. They have already begun to change faculty interactions with each other and with students, and to stimulate ideas about innovative curricular and co-curricular efforts that promise to enhance the community's ability to embrace multiple ways of knowing and being.

A guiding principle in our efforts comes from the work of Parker Palmer: we teach who we are. Our values and our sense of identity are always present, whether we acknowledge them or not. When we believe we can leave them out of the classroom, we are deluding ourselves. We can teach (and live) much better by recognizing their presence and by understanding and honoring them. This helps us to honor our students' values and identities as well, and to create classroom spaces that allow greater freedom in thought and exploration. Such safe spaces are important for our students. They are equally important for us. When we (as Palmer says) join soul and role we avoid the fragmentation of disconnected or compartmentalized living and enjoy the fulfillment of interacting with others as whole individuals.

We wanted to utilize a holistic approach to learning—one in which we value our hearts as well as our minds. By opening the way for faculty to be whole individuals—individuals who, in addition to demonstrating the strength of being knowledgeable and skilled, are also vulnerable learners—we make it possible for students to express their own strengths and vulnerabilities and to appreciate these in others. Whole professors give students permission to be whole individuals in the classroom; we do this with our language and in the ways we model it for them. We encourage students to approach learning with the knowledge that they are valued as people with unique gifts and perspectives, and students then learn to value others for their own gifts and perspectives. Students learn to value honesty and integrity and they develop compassion and tolerance for those who are different from them.

A faculty member in English has offered some thoughts about how the dinners have shaped her teaching:

> The interdisciplinary faculty dinner dialogues at Spelman College inspired me to reconsider my approach to teaching argument. I routinely ask students to imagine an audience for their written arguments, but the faculty dinner dialogues gave me a model for making audience more real for my Argumentation students. Faculty dialogue participants were asked to prepare a list of five people living or dead that they would like to have dinner with. After a lively group discussion about our lists, I wondered how my students might respond to a similar activity. Thus, I took inspiration from this activity to design my own class project called Digital Dinner Dialogues. Students were asked to identify at least four real people, living or dead, and then design a digital dinner dialogue in which they and their guests engaged a controversial social issue. Student projects typically took the form of a dynamic webpage or PowerPoint and included an aural invitation, place cards with biographical sketches, rationales for location, table setting, and

speaking order, and a scripted dialogue between guests based on research. The experience proved so rewarding that it has become the capstone assignment for my Argumentation course.

President Tatum is committed to continuing the Dinner and Dialogue program. We have also spun off a regular program of faculty-hosted dinners to sustain our efforts. After a few dinners, we began to appreciate the openness and connections we were experiencing and to recognize the value of our conversations for the entire campus community. We asked ourselves how we might enable faculty members not seated at the president's dinner table to deepen their sense of community at Spelman and decided to host spin-off dinners led by teams of faculty members from the original Dinner and Dialogue group. Two sets of faculty-led dinners resulted. The faculty members in one of these series were so enthusiastic about their experiences that they named themselves the Lighthouse Community. Members of this spin-off group carried their connection across campus in a significant way. Two department chairs were wrestling with an issue that involved a conflict of interest between the departments. A junior faculty member from each department had participated in the Lighthouse Community dinners. Because of the connection they had experienced in the dinners, they were able to put aside territorial differences as they contemplated the issue. Their open perspectives allowed them to see a way to resolve the conflict that was satisfactory to each of their department chairs. Their connection allowed the problem to dissolve.

A significant factor in this situation is that the faculty members who saw a way out of the conflict were junior faculty, who may have had less attachment to a particular outcome. Our dinners included both junior and senior faculty. While this mix added to the richness of our discussions, it was sometimes problematic. In a situation where a senior and a junior faculty member from the same department were at the table, honesty was more challenging. This was especially true if the senior faculty member was a department chair. The senior faculty member may not have wanted to reveal vulnerabilities and the junior faculty member may have feared consequences for honesty. When planning such a dialogue series, it may be helpful not to have junior and senior faculty members from a single department in the same dialogues.

Another issue we faced was the desire by some participants to identify and work toward clear outcomes early on, while others want to leave the discussions more open ended, so that outcomes would arise organically. We found that the tension between these viewpoints actually aided our dialogues. We struck a delicate balance between simply being with each other and being open to how our discussions could help faculty, students, and the college. In one session, our dialogue developed into a discussion about innovation at Spelman and led to a visioning exercise we conducted individually. An unexpected outcome of that exercise was the establishment of an annual day in which faculty make presentations and hold discussions on teaching.

We plan to hold a retreat for all faculty involved in the dinners with the president and those participating in the faculty-led spin-off dinners to continue the dialogues and our efforts to expand the reach of our interactions across campus. All of the Dinner and Dialogue efforts support the college's goal of helping students to see themselves as global citizens, and to facilitate their ability to interact positively with people who are different from them.

BUILDING COMMUNITY AT COMMUNITY COLLEGES, ONE POEM AT A TIME

Dennis Huffman, Program Supervisor, Prince George's Community College, Hyattsville, Maryland

Fostering connections between faculty can be particularly problematic at community colleges, where so many of the faculty are part-time and spend most of their day off campus. At Prince George's Community College, Dennis Huffman uses poetry as a way to generate meaningful conversation and community among his scattered and isolated faculty.

Community colleges have wonderful missions, and they are places where rolling up one's sleeves and jumping into the work is profoundly meaningful. Faculty members are primarily focused on teaching, and life-long learning is our mantra. The word *community* is in our name, and we take that seriously. But even at community colleges, connectedness does not always come as naturally as we might like.

Here's a sobering fact: According to the Maryland Association of Community Colleges 2008 Databook, of the 7,512 individuals providing credit instruction at the state's sixteen community colleges, more than two-thirds (67.7%) were part-time faculty members. When two-thirds of the instructors do not have offices, aren't expected to participate on committees or attend faculty meetings, and teach mostly evening and weekend classes, building community is challenging, if not downright quixotic.

My own work is at an off-campus center where three-fourths of the more than one hundred instructors are part time. All of these individuals have the required academic background, and each of them comes to work hoping to do a good job, but there are times when the pieces of the teaching and learning puzzle spread out before us just don't seem to fit together. There are times when being a part-time faculty member at an off-campus location is like stepping up to the plate two strikes behind in the count. How can there be meaningful conversations among the faculty when they never see each other? How can there be engagement with the institution without meaningful contact? And, as is the case for some, how can there be commitment to two, three, or even four employers at the same time?

Those questions were weighing heavily on my mind when the wonderful book *Teaching with Fire: Poetry That Sustains the Courage to Teach* came into my life. It contains not only poetry but essays by educators describing why the poems they chose are meaningful to them. The book led me to start sharing weekly poems with the faculty at my site, along with my own comments about why the poem had spoken to me.

I had a vague feeling that if the faculty were to have a shared reading experience it might somehow build a sense of community. I also wanted to insert a bit of art—beauty—into our experience,

Appendix C: Administrative and Campuswide Initiatives

as off-campus employees miss out on the chance to wander through the college art gallery or drop in on a performance. In terms of my comments, it seemed important to keep sending messages of gratitude to the faculty. I wanted to acknowledge the challenges in what they were doing, and remind them of why the work of a community college is so important.

At first, my comments were quite limited. I would say, "I hope you like this" and "Thanks for being here." I was self-conscious and sometimes went begging for morsels of positive feedback from the daytime faculty. I suspected that most of the teachers thought I was crazy and that the whole thing was a waste of paper. I wasn't at all convinced that what I was doing mattered, and I didn't always manage to get a poem into the mailboxes every week. Then, late one afternoon near the end of the semester, in a week when I hadn't managed to get a poem distributed, I bumped into a gruff old math teacher who was getting off the elevator as I was getting on. "Hey!" he snarled. I cringed, but then he said: "Where's my poem? I really need it this week."

That brief encounter was a turning point. It has led to a burgeoning collection of poetry anthologies on my bookshelf and early morning encounters with Garrison Keillor's *Writer's Almanac* on public radio. Here is a sampling of what other faculty members have told me about the poetry:

- The poems allow us to share some common metaphors for what we are about.
- Your sending the poetry builds community simply through the demonstration of willingness to share one's passion.
- It keeps the heart in my daily teaching and reminds me of my values.
- It's useful because it reminds me of my purpose.
- They help me lift my nose up from the grindstone of developmental math.
- I love the poems. I see them as an important contribution to my stress busting and enjoy sharing them with my students.

- It has created a kind of e-community and a knowledge that we are all here for the same reasons.
- I enjoy the poems, and your comments get me thinking. There are times that I feel better about my role in the community college setting and my contributions as a teacher.
- The very act of sending out the poems sends an excellent message to the people who work here. Whether they are into poetry or not, they know that you care about them and your job and that rubs off on people.

So has the project resulted in "transformative conversations" among the adjunct faculty? I don't know. We don't have a water cooler to gather around. (Although someone did suggest that I post each week's poem near the photocopier, since that's a place where people still come together.) I know, however, that sharing these poems has, on occasion, permitted me, and my colleagues, to sip from "the hidden aquifer that feeds human knowing." That's a start.

IS THIS JUST CONVERSATION OR IS SOMETHING GOING TO HAPPEN? A COLLEGEWIDE EXPERIENCE OF INTEGRATED LEARNING

Diana Chapman Walsh, President Emerita, Wellesley College, and Patricia M. Byrne, Administrative Dean, Harvard Divinity School

Often untapped, times of transition can open up possibilities for candid, campuswide conversations. At Wellesley College, the ending of a college president's tenure presented an opportunity to consider what it would mean if the seemingly obvious yet radical concept that "student learning is our top priority" shaped every aspect of the college.

We want to make the case that a carefully designed conversation can break down barriers to candid reflection on core issues of student learning and can itself become an opportunity for integrated learning at the institutional level. The example comes from an unorthodox planning process that ran through the final three years of the Walsh presidency at Wellesley College. As with any process, the context shaped the purpose, and the context changed. What began as the codicil to a five-year fundraising campaign became the closing act of a fourteen-year presidency. At the end of a long cycle of incremental improvements to the college, we wanted to shape an opportunity for the college as a whole to learn from its recent history and to solidify steps it had been taking toward becoming a learning organization.

Our more immediate aims were to prepare the community for a presidential transition, to take stock of what had (and had not) been accomplished, and to draw a deep breath and collect ideas and observations that might otherwise be swept under the rug as the college cleared the way for a new leader.

To accomplish these aims, we set out to mine and sharpen the crucial questions we had been living—resisting the strong temptation to prescribe answers prematurely—trusting that the act of claiming the questions themselves would benefit the presidential search committee, candidates for the presidency, and a new administration during its early formative years. We considered it essential to incorporate a wide range of perspectives across the campus community and to design a process that would be fluid enough to allow for ambiguity, discovery, and dissent and yet structured enough to bind anxiety at a time of uncertainty, and propel forward movement. Our process was in that sense "emergent"; we were inventing it as it unfolded. To help us make sense of what we were seeing, we enlisted the help of outside thinking partners from a variety of planning traditions and disciplines. Some were more helpful than others.

From the outset we were conscious of issues that threatened to derail the expansive thinking we needed from this commission. So we charged two working groups—one on financial management, the other on faculty governance—to create separate spaces for focused problem solving, removing from the commission's ambit all but the bigger questions, which we hoped they would follow wherever the questions might lead. They led to the heart of the matter: to the quality of students' educational experiences, their engagement with their learning, the "aliveness" of it for them, its authenticity, depth, and power, in short, how well-integrated that learning was and might become.

The commission discussed in some detail, and ultimately ratified, the statement that "student learning is our top priority," a conclusion that sounds benign or even banal until you unpack its implications. The aspirations for students to which commissioners gradually gave voice, tentatively at first, became increasingly pointed and poignant as members experienced the shift in consciousness that can occur when people come together to learn from their differences, reveal their disappointments, and reach for a desired future they have imagined together.

One interchange that illustrates this evolution occurred late in the process. While reviewing the commission's draft "points of consensus," a working group member from the faculty snarled: "Is this just conversation or is something going to happen?" As it became clear that whether something would happen was largely contingent on the willingness of faculty members to take up their internal conflicts, the room grew quieter and the conversation slowed and deepened. One faculty member confessed that "we can't even agree on what our students' jobs are here"; another added, "their energies are elsewhere, not in the classroom."

These frustrations triggered an exchange about a general "grumpiness" on the electronic conferences with faculty complaining about students and students about faculty. "We have no collective agreement on what is important," said another faculty member, "no sense of pride at the end of the day (or at the end of a course) that we have achieved something of value. There's a sense in which everything is too much." A feeling of defeat descended on the room.

After a moment, the same professor returned to the commission's statement that student learning should become the college's top priority. "What if decision making and accountability were driven by student learning?" he wondered aloud.

A trustee in the group said, quietly, "The goal would be to find the energy to lift us up."

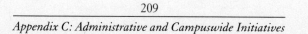

Appendix C: Administrative and Campuswide Initiatives

"Well, that would be exciting," the professor continued, shifting the mood. "We could set some real goals and measure our progress."

This moment crystallized how the simple act of foregrounding student learning could defuse the endless and fruitless debates about whether students were working too hard, or not hard enough. It was liberating to be asking, instead, how *well* they were working; how well *we* were working, what we, *and* they, were actually accomplishing.

We would never have reached that moment, or others like it, without the foundation of trust the commission built over the year. Building the trust required close attention and a constant investment of time in refining the process. Having exceptionally good and smart people in the room was not enough. They needed a process that was being held and cared for, palpably for the group, by a leadership team that continued to believe in it when it faltered, as it inevitably did. Our conversations had ups and downs, times when it was anything but obvious that we were making progress. We had disagreements and unresolved conflicts and a few dispiriting sessions when, despite our best efforts, the discussion meandered or flagged. The leaders had to be willing to take risks and to ask others to bear with us when our plans failed to work out as we hoped they would.

They did bear with us, and, in the end, the commission members were unanimous that if there was a single outcome that would most strengthen the college, it would be a continuation of conversations at the depth theirs had ultimately reached. The widely representative group became progressively more cohesive, developing respect for one another while exercising their stewardship responsibilities for a college they all keenly valued, and yet saw in different ways.

None of this would have been possible had we not assembled a diverse group from many precincts of the college, made the initial distinction between problem solving and conversation, resolved to mine the lessons of our recent history without laying out a blueprint for the future, and diligently worked to sustain a flexible holding environment that engendered a sense of collective responsibility and mutual trust. These conditions enabled the commission to occupy a special space in which members could probe to the core of the student experience, express their unspoken concerns about aspects of the student and faculty cultures, imagine ways in which the college might be letting students down, and voice their heartfelt hopes for the students of the future.

INTEGRATED, EMBEDDED, AND ENGAGED: PROMOTING A CULTURE OF RESPONSIBILITY AT MSU — CHAUTAUQUA/DIALOGUES

Stephen L. Esquith, Professor, Department of Philosophy, and Dean, Residential College in the Arts and Humanities at Michigan State University

Michigan State University's 21st-Century Chautauqua employs a conversational strategy of change in the most fundamental ways possible — simultaneously highlighting the key role that conversation plays in igniting and developing relationships, in pedagogical exploration, and in innovative programs — while also serving as an exemplary model of integrative education.

What is a chautauqua? Originally, the term referred to a nineteenth-century program that brought educational speakers and performers together for families vacationing on the shores of Lake Chautauqua in upstate New York. Quickly, it became synonymous with any open public forum for the discussion of cultural and scientific issues of the day.

The 21st-Century Chautauqua at MSU began with a two-year program of campus dialogues in the three residential colleges — James Madison, Lyman Briggs, and the Residential College in the Arts and Humanities (RCAH) — cosponsored by the Association of American Colleges and Universities to build a culture of individual, social, and institutional responsibility.

Why campus dialogues on responsibility? The great virtue of American colleges and universities is the value they place on academic freedom: the freedom to explore and discover new knowledge and to debate conventional wisdom. This is not merely an intercollegiate sport; academic freedom is absolutely necessary if we are to address the problems and challenges of our times. As trite as it may sound, there is no disputing the fact that without these spaces for free inquiry and open discussion, we would not have the human resources—the next generation of scientists and poets of every stripe—that we need to meet challenges as different as global warming, malaria, and child abuse and neglect.

We also know, however, that for a college or university to function productively, our commitment to academic freedom must be matched by an equally strong sense of personal, social, and institutional responsibility. Rights and responsibilities are opposite sides of the same coin. One cannot effectively enjoy freedom of inquiry in the laboratory, the classroom, the gallery, or the field without a set of agreed-upon community standards. For these standards to be accepted, all the members of the community must feel and take responsibility for them. In the RCAH, for example, who will decide what can and cannot be performed in public? What can and cannot be published on a blog on the college website? What can and cannot be hung on our gallery walls or installed in an outdoor space?

There is no reason to expect unanimous agreement on issues such as these. There is also no reason to wait until a disagreement escalates into an acrimonious exchange, or worse. The skills we need to discuss these difficult questions can be honed before things come to an irreconcilable head. By organizing campus dialogues among students, faculty, and staff who feel strongly about such issues, we make it more likely that we can hold difficult conversations about them.

The 21st-Century Chautauqua student and faculty facilitators work with student groups and organizations to move gradually and naturally to this level of dialogue in which the subject of personal and social responsibility can be achieved. In the RCAH this means actually creating the student organization and governance system that we believe will provide the best institutional structure for campus dialogues.

Another dimension of the 21st-Century Chautauqua, building on what we learn from the campus dialogue project, is to create a range of curricular and co-curricular projects that will institutionalize some of the ideas agreed upon in the local dialogues. In spring 2008, the first 21st-Century MSU Traveling Chautauqua on Sustainability and Human Rights met weekly with students from James Madison, Lyman Briggs, and the RCAH. In fall 2009, a second Traveling Chautauqua on Race, Justice, and Equality met, with the addition of students from the Honors College and other units, in the same weekly format. MSU President Lou Anna K. Simon attended one session on how MSU is addressing this large subject at the institutional level. The fall 2009 series culminated in a three-hour session in which the Spike Lee film *Do the Right Thing* was shown, followed by a discussion. Members of other student organizations, including the W. E. B. DuBois Society in James Madison, participated and indicated a desire to be part of the Chautauqua on race and justice in spring 2009.

Students who have participated in Chautauqua dialogues report a broad range of positive experiences:

- "Participating in the Chautauqua has broadened my perspective, especially when it comes to problem solving. I don't know when I'll ever get the chance again to hear from so many different disciplines at the same time. I know my experiences have allowed me to expand my own critical thinking and communication skills." —Melissa Clark (senior)

- "Even though usually I only participate in our weekly Chautauqua by listening, I feel like those two hours can be some of the most rewarding in my week. I spend all day debating political theory with other social scientists, but Chautauqua is a way for me to explore completely different view points of the same topics. It rounds out my studies, and helps me to connect what I'm thinking about in the abstract to what is going on in the world around me. Chautauqua is the time during the week when instead of trying to prove a point or win a debate, I'm attempting to put together increasingly expanding perspectives on the topic in order to more fully understand what is actually being discussed. While we don't always agree, the guidelines under which we participate foster respect and promote the acknowledgment, if not acceptance, of different opinions."—Joan Campau (senior)

- "The greatest gift Chautauqua gives to students is its egalitarian spirit. Professors are no longer experts with all the correct answers, but individuals with unique life experiences and outlooks. Students and professors come together to learn from each other and work together towards greater mutual understanding."—Rebecca Farnum (first-year student)

- "The most valuable lesson I have learned from Chautauqua is that in a real conversation, the most effective way of presenting your point is by listening to the words other people have to say. When people from different backgrounds come together, they bring totally different sets of knowledge and experience to the dialogue. By listening, you can realize where other people are deriving their arguments from, and then feed them additional or corrected information that might help to shift their point of view. But ultimately, your information and point of view might also be based on faulty ground, and you must be willing to accept that. True Chautauqua helps those involved to realize everyone has something important to say, and that all participants in a dialogue must be viewed as equal if a true mutual understanding is to be attained."—Matthew Swartz (first-year student)

As the project continues to develop and expand, dialogues will become more fully integrated into the undergraduate learning experience, our general education curriculum, and the integrative learning programs at MSU—and, subsequently, more deeply embedded in our institutional culture. These projects include new service-learning, field experience, internship, and civic engagement courses; new study abroad and more local study away programs with a service-learning or civic engagement component; and new trans-college courses on professional and civic responsibility. To facilitate ongoing discussion of Chautauqua issues, a 21st-Century Chautauqua wiki, http://www.21c-chautauqua.org/wiki, was established. The wiki adopts the guiding principles of the dialogues to this digital medium and takes advantage of the technology to help us understand other perspectives and appreciate the complexities of today's issues.

Through participation in the Chautauqua dialogues, MSU students become agents of their own integrative education, learning as they interact with and explore new ideas and perspectives. The success of the ongoing conversation rests squarely on the active and engaged participation of the learning community—a prerequisite deliberately built in to the program. Overall, the 21st-Century Chautauqua at MSU serves as a promising model for one way in which we can shift the focus of undergraduate education to incorporate a fundamental emphasis on student engagement and responsibility.

Notes

FOREWORD

1. Diana Chapman Walsh, "Trustworthy Leadership: Can We Be the Leaders We Need Our Students to Become?" (keynote address, Institute on College Student Values, Florida State University, Tallahassee, FL, February 4, 2005).
2. Blair A. Ruble, "The Challenges of the Twenty-First Century City" (Fetzer-Wilson Center Seminar: Community Resilience in the Twenty-First Century, December 2008).
3. The Dalai Lama (The Balance of Mind-Heart Education conference, University of British Columbia, Vancouver, Canada, 2004).

INTRODUCTION

1. Wendell Berry, "The Loss of the University," *Home Economics* (San Francisco: North Point Press, 1987), p. 77.
2. Harry Lewis, *Excellence Without a Soul: Does Liberal Education Have a Future?* (New York: Public Affairs, 2007), p. xv.
3. Lewis, *Excellence Without a Soul*, p. xiv.
4. Lewis, *Excellence Without a Soul*, p. 18.
5. Anthony T. Kronman, *Education's End: Why Our Colleges and Universities Have Given Up on the Meaning of Life* (New Haven, CT: Yale University Press, 2007), p. 6.

6. Kronman, *Education's End,* p. 6.
7. See http://www.couragerenewal.org.
8. For information on the Fetzer Institute, see http://www.fetzer.org.
9. Alain de Lille (Alanus de Insulis), *Anticlaudianus: The Good and Perfect Man,* trans. James J. Sheridan (Toronto: Pontifical Institute of Medieval Studies, 1973).
10. Mary Taylor Huber, Cheryl Brown, Pat Hutchings, Richard Gale, Ross Miller, and Molly Breen, eds., "Integrative Learning: Opportunities to Connect," Public Report of the Integrative Learning Project sponsored by the Association of American Colleges and Universities and The Carnegie Foundation for the Advancement of Teaching, Stanford, CA (January 2007), http://www.carnegiefoundation.org/elibrary/ integrativelearning (accessed December 7, 2009).
11. Deborah DeZure, Marcia Babb, and Stephanie Waldmann, "Integrative Learning Nationwide: Emerging Themes and Practices," *peerReview* (Summer/Fall, 2005), p. 28.
12. American Association of Colleges and Universities, Conference announcement for "Integrative Learning: Addressing the Complexities" (October 22–24, 2009), http://www.aacu.org/meetings/integrative _learning/index.cfm.
13. Association of American Colleges and Universities and The Carnegie Foundation for the Advancement of Teaching, "Integrative Learning: Opportunities to Connect," http://gallery.carnegiefoundation.org/ ilp/index.htm (accessed December 7, 2009).
14. Mary Huber, and Pat Hutchings, *Integrative Learning: Mapping the Terrain* (Washington, DC: AAC&U, 2004), p. 13; also at http://www .aacu.org/integrative_learning/pdfs/ILP_Statement.pdf.
15. Sean Esbjörn-Hargens, Jonathan Reams, and Olen Gunnlaugson, *Integral Education* (Albany, NY: SUNY Press, 2010).
16. Aurobindo Ghose, *The Essential Aurobindo*, edited and introduced by Robert McDermott (Great Barrington, MA: SteinerBooks, 2001). Ken Wilber, *A Brief History of Everything,* 2nd edition (Boulder, CO: Shambala, 2007).
17. Martin Buber, *I and Thou*, trans. Walter Kaufmann (New York: Free Press, 1971).
18. C. Otto Scharmer, *Theory U: Leading from the Future as It Emerges* (Cambridge, MA: SoL, 2007), pp. 250ff.

CHAPTER 1: TOWARD A PHILOSOPHY
OF INTEGRATIVE EDUCATION

1. Andrew Carroll, *Letters of a Nation* (New York: Broadway Books, 1999), p. 240.
2. Kenneth Grahame, *The Wind in the Willows* (New York: Signet Classics, 2006), p. 9.
3. Michael Polanyi, *Personal Knowledge* (Chicago: University of Chicago Press, 1960).
4. Stephen H. Blackwell, *The Quill and the Scalpel* (Columbus, OH: The Ohio State University Press, 2009), p. xii.
5. Ian Barbour, *Religion in an Age of Science* (San Francisco: HarperSan-Francisco, 1990), p. 220.
6. Barbour, *Religion*, p. 221.
7. Gary Zukav, *The Dancing Wu Li Masters* (New York: Morrow, 1979), p. 94. Original source: Henry Stapp, "S-Matrix Interpretation of Quantum Theory," Lawrence Berkeley Laboratory preprint, June 22, 1970 (revised edition: *Physical Review*, D3, 1971, 1303).
8. Polanyi, *Personal Knowledge*.
9. Dr. James Shapiro, University of Chicago, quoted in "Dr. Barbara McClintock, 90, Gene Research Pioneer Dies," *New York Times* (September 4, 1992), p. C16.
10. Evelyn Fox Keller, *A Feeling for the Organism: The Life and Work of Barbara McClintock* (New York: Freeman, 1983), p. 198.
11. Sue V. Rosser, "The Gender Equation," *The Sciences* (September/October 1992), p. 46.
12. Evelyn Fox Keller, *Reflections on Gender and Science* (New Haven: Yale University Press, 1985), p. 164.

CHAPTER 2: WHEN PHILOSOPHY
IS PUT INTO PRACTICE

1. Konnilyn G. Feig, *Hitler's Death Camps: The Sanity of Madness* (New York: Holmes & Meier, 1979), p. 57.
2. Fyodor Dostoevsky, *The Brothers Karamazov* (New York: Barnes & Noble Classics, 2004), p. 58.

3. Candace B. Pert, *Molecules of Emotion: The Science behind Mind-Body Medicine* (New York: Simon & Schuster, 1999).
4. Sheila Tobias, *Overcoming Math Anxiety* (New York: Norton, 1995).
5. Uri Treisman, "Studying Students Studying Calculus: A Look at the Lives of Minority Mathematics Students in College," *College Mathematics Journal* 23, no. 5 (November 1992).
6. "Carnegie Academy for the Scholarship of Teaching and Learning," Carnegie Foundation for the Advancement of Teaching, http://www.carnegiefoundation.org/scholarship-teaching-learning.
7. Anthony Bryk and Barbara Schneider, *Trust in Schools: A Core Resource for Improvement* (New York: Russell Sage Foundation, 2004).
8. Lisa Miller, "Belief Watch," *Newsweek* (January 22, 2007), http://www.newsweek.com/id/70063.
9. Miller, "Belief Watch."
10. James Freedman, "Lessons from Illness," *Dartmouth Medicine* (Fall 1994), p. 15.

CHAPTER 3: BEYOND THE DIVIDED
ACADEMIC LIFE

1. Anthony T. Kronman, *Education's End: Why Our Colleges and Universities Have Given Up on the Meaning of Life* (New Haven, CT: Yale University Press, 2007). Harry Lewis, *Excellence Without a Soul: Does Liberal Education Have a Future?* (New York: Public Affairs, 2007), p. 259.
2. Ralph Waldo Emerson, "Experience," in *Ralph Waldo Emerson: Selected Essays* (1844; New York: Penguin, 1982), p. 289.
3. Derek Bok, *Our Underachieving Colleges* (Princeton, NJ: Princeton University Press, 2006), p. 40.
4. Bok, *Our Underachieving Colleges*, pp. 40–41.
5. Alfred North Whitehead, *The Aims of Education* (1929; New York: Free Press, 1967), pp. 93–100.
6. Albert Einstein, "Principles of Research" (address for Max Planck's sixtieth birthday, Physical Society, Berlin, Germany, 1918), http://www.cs.ucla.edu/~slu/on_research/einstein_essay2.html (accessed February 2009).
7. Albert Einstein, "What Life Means to Einstein: An Interview by George Sylvester Viereck," *Saturday Evening Post* 202 (October 26, 1929), p. 117.
8. Henri Poincaré, "Mathematical Definitions in Education," in *Insights of Genius* (New York: Springer Verlag, 1996), p. 351.

9. Whitehead, *Aims of Education*, pp. 1–2.

10. John Keats, Letter to George and Thomas Keats of December 22, 1817, in *The Complete Poetical Works of John Keats*, ed. H. E. Scudder (Boston: Riverside Press, 1899), p. 277.

11. Arthur O. Lovejoy, *The Great Chain of Being: A Study of the History of an Idea: The William James Lectures Delivered at Harvard University, 1933* (Cambridge, MA: Harvard University Press, 1936).

12. Robert N. Bellah, Richard Madsen, William M. Sullivan, Ann Swidler, and Steven M. Tipton, *The Good Society* (New York: Vintage, 1992), p. 44.

13. Arthur Zajonc, ed., *The New Physics and Cosmology: Dialogues with the Dalai Lama* (New York: Oxford University Press, 2004).

14. David Bohm, *The Special Theory of Relativity* (New York: Benjamin, 1965), p. 148.

15. Werner Heisenberg, *Physicist's Conception of Nature*, trans. Arnold J. Ponerans (New York: Harcourt, Brace, 1958), p. 24.

16. Niels Bohr, *The Philosophical Writings of Niels Bohr*, vol. 3, *Essays 1958–1962 on Atomic Physics and Human Knowledge* (Woodbridge, CT: Ox Bow Press, 1963), pp. 4, 72.

17. Anton Zeilinger, "Why the Quantum?" in *Science and Ultimate Reality: Quantum Theory, Cosmology, and Complexity,* ed. John Barrows, P. C. W. Davies, and Charles L. Harper (Cambridge: Cambridge University Press, 2004), pp. 218–219.

18. Francisco J. Varela, *Sleeping, Dreaming, and Dying* (Boston: Wisdom, 1997), p. 1.

19. B. Alan Wallace, *The Taboo of Subjectivity: Toward a New Science of Consciousness* (New York: Oxford University Press, 2000).

20. Francisco J. Varela, Evan Thompson, and Eleanor Rosch, *The Embodied Mind* (Cambridge, MA: MIT Press, 1992). Evan Thompson, *Mind in Life* (Cambridge, MA: Harvard University Press, 2007).

21. William James, *The Principles of Psychology* (1890; New York: Dover, 1950), p. 424.

22. See the Association for Contemplative Mind in Higher Education for resources: http://www.acmhe.org.

23. Laurent A. Parks Daloz, Cheryl H. Keen, James P. Keen, and Sharon Daloz Parks, *Common Fire: Leading Lives of Commitment in a Complex World* (Boston: Beacon Press, 1996). Sharon Parks, *Big Questions, Worthy Dreams* (San Francisco: Jossey-Bass, 2000).

CHAPTER 4: ATTENDING TO INTERCONNECTION, LIVING THE LESSON

1. Dalai Lama, *Washington Post* (October 21, 2007), p. B1.
2. Albert Einstein, Nathan Rosen, and Boris Podolsky, "Can Quantum-Mechanical Description of Reality Be Considered Complete?" *Physical Review* 47, no. 10 (1935), pp. 777–780.
3. George Greenstein and Arthur Zajonc, *The Quantum Challenge*, 2nd ed. (Salisbury, MA: Jones & Bartlett, 2005).
4. Philip W. Anderson, "More Is Different," *Science* 177 (August 4, 1972), pp. 393–396.
5. Robert Laughlin, *A Different Universe: Reinventing Physics from the Bottom Down* (New York: Basic Books, 2005), p. 221.
6. Arthur Zajonc, *Catching the Light: The Entwined History of Light and Mind* (New York: Oxford University Press, 1993).
7. Paul Hawken, Amory Lovins, and L. Hunter Lovins, *Natural Capitalism: Creating the Next Industrial Revolution* (Boston: Little, Brown, 1999).
8. Stephen Marglin, *The Dismal Science: How Thinking Like an Economist Undermines Community* (Cambridge, MA: Harvard University Press, 2008), p. 263.
9. Joseph Henrich, Robert Boyd, Samuel Bowles, Colin Camerer, Ernst Fehr, Herbert Gintis, and Richard McElreath, "In Search of Homo Economicus: Behavioral Experiments in 15 Small-Scale Societies," *American Economic Review* 91 (2001), pp. 73–78.
10. Henrich et al., "In Search."
11. Daniel Goleman, *Ecological Intelligence* (New York: Random House, 2009).
12. *Sandy C. Marks, Jr. DDS, PhD: Collected Memories from Friends, Students and Colleagues* (University of Massachusetts, n.d.), p. 7, http://www.umassmed.edu/uploadedfiles/marksbook.pdf.
13. *Sandy C. Marks, Jr.*, p. 15.
14. John Keats, Letter to George and Thomas Keats of December 22, 1817, in *The Complete Poetical Works of John Keats*, ed. H. E. Scudder (Boston: Riverside Press, 1899), p. 277.
15. Ralph Waldo Emerson, *Ralph Waldo Emerson: Selected Essays* (1844; New York: Penguin, 1982), p. 274.
16. Evelyn Fox Keller, *A Feeling for the Organism* (New York: Times Books, 1984), pp. 200–204.

17. Arthur Zajonc, *Meditation as Contemplative Inquiry* (Great Barrington, MA: Lindisfarne Press, 2009).

18. Rainer Maria Rilke, *Letters to a Young Poet,* trans. R. Snell (1903; New York: Dover, 2002), p. 45.

19. Johann Wolfgang von Goethe, *Scientific Studies*, ed. and trans. D. Miller (1821; New York: Suhrkamp, 1988), p. 307.

20. Erwin Schrödinger, *Mind and Matter* (1958; Cambridge: Cambridge University Press, 1967).

21. Pierre Hadot, *What Is Ancient Philosophy?* trans. M. Chase (Cambridge, MA: Harvard University Press, 2002), pp. 274, xiii.

22. Maurice Merleau-Ponty, *Phenomenology of Perception*, trans. C. Smith (London: Routledge, 1962), preface.

23. Goethe, *Scientific Studies*, p. 39.

24. Keller, *A Feeling*, p. 200.

25. Douglas Sloan, *Insight-Imagination* (Westport, CT: Greenwood Press, 1993). Robert J. Sternberg and Janet E. Davidson, *The Nature of Insight* (Cambridge, MA: MIT Press, 1995).

26. Simone Weil, *Gravity and Grace,* trans. E. Crawford (New York: Routledge, 2002).

27. Ralph Waldo Emerson, *The Complete Works of Ralph Waldo Emerson*, Centenary Edition, vol. 8, *Letters and Social Aims*, ed. Edward Waldo Emerson (1875; Boston: Houghton Mifflin, 1903–1904), p. 365.

CHAPTER 5: EXPERIENCE, CONTEMPLATION, AND TRANSFORMATION

1. William G. Perry, Jr., *Forms of Intellectual and Ethical Development in the College Years: A Scheme* (Austin, TX: Holt, Rinehart, and Winston, 1970). Jack Mezirow, *Learning as Transformation* (San Francisco: Jossey-Bass, 2000). Robert Kegan, *The Evolving Self: Problem and Process in Human Development* (Cambridge, MA: Harvard University Press, 1982). Robert Kegan, *In Over Our Heads: The Mental Demands of Modern Life* (Cambridge, MA: Harvard University Press, 1994). Lawrence Kohlberg, *The Philosophy of Moral Development: Important Stages and the Idea of Justice* (San Francisco: Harper & Row, 1981). Sharon Parks, *Big Questions, Worthy Dreams* (San Francisco: Jossey-Bass, 2000). Ken Wilber, *The Essential Ken Wilber* (Boston: Shambala, 1998).

2. Jane M. Healy, *Endangered Minds* (New York: Simon & Schuster, 1999).

3. Sharon Begley, *Train Your Mind, Change Your Brain* (New York: Ballantine, 2007).

4. Kegan, *In Over Our Heads*, p. 188.

5. Patricia M. King and Marcia B. Baxter Magolda, "A Developmental Perspective on Learning," *Journal of College Student Development* 37 (1996), pp. 163–173.

6. Kegan, *In Over Our Heads*, p. 351.

7. Evan Thompson, "Empathy and Consciousness," *Journal of Consciousness Studies* 8 (2001), pp. 1–32.

8. Daniel Goleman, *Social Intelligence: The New Science of Human Relationships* (New York: Bantam, 2006).

9. Elliot Turiel, "An Experimental Test of the Sequentiality of the Developmental Stage in the Child's Development of Moral Judgments," *Journal of Personality and Social Psychology* 3, no. 6 (1966), pp. 611–618.

10. Thomas S. Kuhn, *The Structure of Scientific Revolutions* (Chicago: University of Chicago Press, 1970).

11. Rainer Maria Rilke, *Letters to a Young Poet,* trans. R. Snell (1903; New York: Dover, 2002), p. 21.

12. Johann Wolfgang Goethe, "Maximen und Reflexionen," no. 509, *Werke* (Hamburg edition), vol. 7, ed. E. Trunz (Munich, Germany: C. Wegner, 1981), p. 435. For more on Goethean science and its educational implications, see the work of Craig Holdrege at http://www.nature institute.org.

13. Johann Wolfgang Goethe, *Briefwechsel zwischen Goethe und F. H. Jacobi*, ed. M. Jacobi (Leipzig, Germany: Weidmann, 1846), p. 198.

14. Paul Cézanne, *Paul Cézanne Letters*, ed. J. Rewald, trans. M. Kay (Cambridge, MA: De Capo, 1995), p. 306.

15. Helga Kuhse and Peter Singer, *Should Baby Live? The Problem of Handicapped Infants* (New York: Oxford University Press, 1985).

16. Cornelius Pietzner, ed., *A Candle on the Hill: Images of Camphill Life* (Edinburgh, Scotland: Floris Books, 1990).

17. Alfred North Whitehead, *The Aims of Education* (1929; New York: Free Press, 1967), p. 2.

18. For an article about Joel Upton, see Leanna James, "Eros and Insight," *Amherst Magazine* (Spring 2004), http://www3.amherst.edu/magazine/ issues/04spring/eros_insight/index.html. C. Dustin and Joanna Ziegler, *Practicing Mortality: Art, Philosophy, and Contemplative Seeing* (New York: Palgrave Macmillan, 2005).

19. Arthur Zajonc, "Love and Knowledge: Recovering the Heart of Learning through Contemplation," *Teacher's College Record,* Special Issue on Contemplative Practices and Education 108, no. 9 (September 2006): 1742–1759. Arthur Zajonc, "Science and Spirituality: Finding the Right Map," in *Integrative Learning and Action: a Call to Wholeness*, ed. S. M. Awbrey, D. Dana, V. W. Miller, P. Robinson, M. M. Ryan, and D. K. Scott, (New York: Peter Lang, 2006) pp. 57–80. Arthur Zajonc, *Meditation as Contemplative Inquiry* (Great Barrington, MA: Lindisfarne Press, 2009).

20. John Gravois, "Meditate on It: Can Adding Contemplation to the Classroom Lead Students to More Eureka Moments?"*Chronicle of Higher Education* 52, no. 9 (October 21, 2005), p. A10. Association for Contemplative Mind in Higher Education website, http://www .acmhe.org.

21. Arthur W. Chickering, John C. Dalton, and Liesa Stamm, *Encouraging Authenticity and Spirituality in Higher Education* (San Francisco, CA: Jossey-Bass, 2006).

22. Higher Education Research Institute (HERI), UCLA, "Spiritual Changes in Students during the Undergraduate Years," news release, December 18, 2007, http://spirituality.ucla.edu/news/Spirituality_on _Campus_release_12.18.07.pdf.

23. HERI, UCLA, "Spiritual Changes," p. 5.

24. Higher Education Research Institute, UCLA, "College Students Report High Levels of Spirituality and Religiousness," news release, April 13, 2005, http://spirituality.ucla.edu/spirituality/news/release_study3.pdf.

25. Larry Braskamp, Lois Calian Trautvetter, and Kelly Ward, *Putting Students First: How Colleges Develop Students Purposefully* (Bolton, MA: Anker, 2006).

26. Higher Education Research Institute, UCLA, "Strong Majority of College and University Faculty Identify Themselves as Spiritual," news release, February 28, 2006, http://spirituality.ucla.edu/news/faculty _report_release.pdf.

27. Arthur Zajonc, "Molding the Self, Common Cognitive Sources of Science and Religion," in *Education as Transformation*, ed. V. H. Kazanjian, Jr. and P. L. Laurence, pp. 59–68 (New York: Peter Lang, 2000). Arthur Zajonc, "Spirituality in Higher Education: Overcoming the Divide," *Liberal Education* 89, no. 1 (Winter 2003), pp. 50–58. Arthur Zajonc, "Science and Spirituality: Finding the Right Map," in *Integrative Learning and Action: A Call to Wholeness*, eds.

S. M. Awbrey, D. Dana, V. W. Miller, P. Robinson, M. M. Ryan, and D. K. Scott (New York: Peter Lang, 2006), pp. 57–80.

28. Stephen Jay Gould, *Rocks of Ages* (New York: Ballantine, 1999).

29. William James, *Essays in Radical Empiricism* (New York: Longmans, Green, 1912), p. 42.

30. William James, *Pluralistic Universe* (1909; New York, Longmans, Green, 1920), p. 314.

31. Alfred North Whitehead, "Religion and Science," *Atlantic Monthly* (August 1925), p. 6, http://www.theatlantic.com/doc/print/192508/whitehead.

32. Anthony T. Kronman, *Education's End: Why Our Colleges and Universities Have Given Up the Meaning of Life* (New Haven, CT: Yale University Press, 2007).

CHAPTER 6: TRANSFORMATIVE CONVERSATIONS ON CAMPUS

1. For information on the Highlander Research and Education Center today, see http://www.highlandercenter.org/. For historical information on the Highlander Folk School, see http://en.wikipedia.org/wiki/Highlander_Folk_School.

2. For information on Princeton Project 55, see http://www.project55.org/.

3. Princeton Project 55, http://www.project55.org/.

4. Myles Horton, *The Long Haul* (New York: Doubleday, 1990), p. 190.

5. Sharon Daloz Parks, *Big Questions, Worthy Dreams* (San Francisco: Jossey-Bass, 2000).

6. Anthony Bryk and Barbara Schneider, *Trust in Schools: A Core Resource for Improvement* (New York: Russell Sage Foundation, 2004).

7. See Parker J. Palmer, *A Hidden Wholeness: The Journey Toward an Undivided Life* (San Francisco: Jossey-Bass, 2004), for an extensive and detailed treatment of such ground rules.

8. Nelle Morton, *The Journey Is Home* (Boston: Beacon Press, 1985), pp. 55–56.

9. Palmer, *A Hidden Wholeness*.

10. *Online Etymology Dictionary*, s.v. "school (1)," http://www.etymonline.com/index.php?search=school&searchmode=none.

11. Abraham Flexner, *Universities: American, English, German* (New York: Oxford University Press, 1930), p. 267.

12. Leanna James, "Eros and Insight," *Amherst Magazine* (Spring 2004), http://www3.amherst.edu/magazine/issues/04spring/eros_insight.

13. Arthur Zajonc, "Love and Knowledge: Recovering the Heart of Learning through Contemplation," *Teacher's College Record* Special Issue on Contemplative Practices and Education 108, no. 9 (September 2006), pp. 1742–1759; also published in *Journal of Cognitive Affective Learning* 3, no. 1 (Fall 2006), pp. 1–9, http://www.jcal.emory.edu/viewarticle .php?id=82&layout=html (accessed December 7, 2009). Arthur Zajonc, "Spirituality in Higher Education: Overcoming the Divide," *Liberal Education*, Journal of the American Association of Colleges and Universities 89, no. 1 (Winter 2003), pp. 50–58. A. W. Chickering, J. C. Dalton, and L. Stamm, *Encouraging Authenticity and Spirituality in Higher Education* (San Francisco, CA: Jossey-Bass, 2006).

14. On Camp Obama, see http://www.huffingtonpost.com/zack-exley/ obama-field-organizers-pl_b_61918.html and http://www .huffingtonpost.com/zack-exley/stories-and-numbers-a-c_b_62278.html.

15. On Marshall Ganz, see http://en.wikipedia.org/wiki/Marshall_Ganz and http://www.hks.harvard.edu/about/faculty-staff-directory/ marshall-ganz.

Index

Handler, A., 97
Hanh, T. N., 86
Harrington, J., 183
Hart Leadership Program in the
    Terry Sanford Institute of Public
    Policy at Duke University, 88,
    165
Harvey, W., 87
Haskell, D., 115, 162–163
Haynes, D. J., 178–181
Heisenberg, W., 11, 66, 68
Hidden curriculum, 26
Higgins, D., x
Higher education: academic alien-
    ation, 157–158; academic in-
    quiries, 49; conversation about the
    heart of, 3–4; institutional change,
    20–21; and messiness of real
    life, 38–39; modes of knowing,
    21–23; requirements for renew-
    ing the heart of, 12; spirituality in,
    115–117; transformative power of
    true education, 101–102
Higher Education Research Institute
    (HERI) at UCLA, 115–116, 118
Highlander Folk Center, 132, 134
Highlander Folk School, 126, 135;
    conversations, 152–153
Hitler's Death Camps (Feig), 38
Homo economicus, 82
Horton, M., 135, 146–147
Hospitable space, 135
Huffman, D., 129, 204–207
Human knowing, roots of, 22
Humanity, 1

I

I-Thou relationship, 12
Imagination, fostering, 93–98

Imaginative insight stage, epistemol-
    ogy of love, 96–97
Imaginative knowing, 106
Impersonal economic transactions,
    82
Indians of the Six Nations treaty
    negotiations, 19–20
"Inner science," 71–72
Inquiry, scholars and, 132–133
Integrative education: brief history
    of, 6–10; and communal reality,
    27; conversations and student
    learning, 207–211; critiques of,
    23; and emotions, 40–42; learn-
    ing/teaching characteristics, 9–10;
    messiness of, 36–40; modes of
    knowing, 21–23; philosoph-
    ical infrastructure of, 22–23;
    and renewing the academy, 14;
    toward a philosophy of, 19–33;
    weak philosophical foundations,
    23–33
Integrative Learning Concept Map
    (Kemp), 9
"Integrative Learning: Opportuni-
    ties to Connect" project, 7–8
Integrative pedagogy, 23, 32
Intentional teaching, 89–93
Intentionality, maintaining in the
    midst of real-world messiness, 40
Interbeing, use of term, 86
Interconnectedness, 77–99; compas-
    sion, awakening, 98–99; emerg-
    ing wholes, 78–81; epistemology,
    enriching, 93–98; imagination,
    fostering, 93–98; intentional
    teaching, 89–93; interdisciplinar-
    ity, 89–93; pedagogies of experi-
    ence and, 81–89

157–158; cell phone use, 158; connections, understanding, 159–160; "Hallelujah Chorus," 160–161; impact on students, 160; knitters, 161; listening to self, 158–159; Tonglin practice, 160–161

Music and meditation in the classroom, 157–173

Global Engagement (VISAGE), 183

Service Opportunities in Leadership (SOL) (Duke University), 88, 165–169; Border Crossing: Leadership, Value Conflicts, and Public Life course, 167–169; interns, 166; service work, 166; Social Issue Investigation Portfolio, 166–167

Shadow work: use of term, 10

Shields, S., 182

Shimony, A., 66

Should Baby Live? The Problem of Handicapped Infants (Kuhse/Singer), 110

Simeon (saint), 29

Simplicius, 96

Singer, P., 110

Skillful Means and the Marketplace course (Barbezat), 164

Social field, and new sciences, 12

Socialized Mind, 103, 106

Socrates, 49

Specialization, and disconnection, 91–92

Spelman College President and Faculty Dinners, 129, 200–204; Dinner and Dialogue program, 201–203; and teaching, 202–203

Spirituality: cognitively oriented, 121; defined, 48; in higher education, 115–117; and the professoriate, 118–122

Stakeholders, use of term, 129

Stamm, L., 146

Stapp, H., 26

Steiner, R., 55, 119

Storytelling, 139

Subbiondo, J., xvii, 5

Sullivan, W. M., 63

Swartz, M., 214

Swidler, A., 63

T

Tacit knowledge, 22

Tatum, B., 129, 201, 203

Theme dorms, 175–178; defined, 175; Religion and Life, 176–177

Thompson, E., 72

Tipton, S. M., 63

Tobias, S., 41–42, 44

Tocqueville, A. de, xiii

Trajectory, maintaining in the midst of real-world messiness, 40

Transformation, pedagogies of, 105–108

Transformation stage, epistemology of love, 95–96

Transformational education movement, xi

Transformative conversations, 125fn; hosting, 136–141; moving from stories to ideas, 141–146; moving to action, 146–149; moving toward, 131–136; student involvement in, 130

Transformative learning, 107

Transformative power of true education, 101

Trautvetter, L. C., 117, 169–173

Treisman, U., 43–44

Trust in Schools (Bryk/Schneider), 46

Turiel, 105

Tutu, Desmond, 78

U

Ultimatum Game, 83–84

Uncovering the Heart of Higher Education conference (San Francisco, 2007), x, xvii, 4, 5, 12–13, 162; Palmer's keynote lecture, 15

Upton, J., 109–110, 113, 135, 146

Urban and Community Design and Contemplative Environmental Design Practice course (Grant), 162

V

Valente, A., 188–191

Values, 152, 165

Varela, F., 72

Varieties of Religious Experience (James), 119–120

Vesalius, A., 86–87

"VP Is In" practice, 195–197; and positive student culture, 197

Vulnerability stage, epistemology of love, 95

W

Wallace, A., 72, 119

Walsh, D. C., ix, 144, 207–211

Ward, K., 117, 169–173

Wave-particle duality, and relationship between question and phenomenon, 80

Weak philosophical foundations, 23–33; epistemological necessity, 27–29; ethical corrective, 31–33; ontological reality, 25–26; pedagogical asset, 29–31

Weil, S., 96

What Is Ancient Philosophy? (Hadot), 96

Whitehead, A. N., 57–58, 60, 113, 120–121

Wilber, K., 8–10, 102, 119

Wind in the Willows (Grahame), 21

Z

Zajonc, A. G., ix, xiv–xv, xvii, xx–xxi, 3–4, 15–16, 53, 77, 101, 126–127, 134–135, 146, 151; educational background, 4

Zajonc-Upton courses, 146

Zeilinger, A., 69

Zeppos, N., 183

Ziegler, J., 113, 164